Free Your Mind

The Four Directions System of Mindfulness ™

by

Anthony Stultz, Ed.D

**The Center for Mindful Living
The Blue Lotus School of Mindfulness Arts**

mindfullivingtoday.com

dragonflymindfulsolutions@gmail.com

Anthony Stultz - copyright © 2017

Cover Photo by Evan Stultz

Table of Contents

Preface ... 3

Foreword ... 4

Introduction ... 6

Chapter One: *The Five Stages: How the Ego Came to Be ... 8*

Chapter Two: *The First Direction: Rediscovering the True Self ... 15*

Chapter Three: *The Second Direction: Understanding the Ego Self ... 24*

Chapter Four: *The Third Direction: Harnessing the Power of the True Self ... 40*

Chapter Five: *The Fourth Direction: Trusting in the True Self ... 48*

Chapter Six: *The Four Directions: A Living Mandala ... 51*

Chapter Seven: *Coming Full Circle ... 60*

Who is Tony? ...61

Preface

The book you are about to read is the result of over thirty years of my professional work in helping individuals, groups and companies experience a positive transformation of their lives and communities.

The Four Directions System developed using the foundational wisdom teachings of meditation and mindfulness while integrating and transliterating via the language and insights of Western psychotherapeutic practices. In 1999 I founded the Blue Lotus School of Mindful Arts and in 2004, I formed the Center for Mindful Living as creative mediums for my students to explore and experience this novel approach to developing clarity, connection and creativity. Discovering what worked for people in times of great stress, such as in prisons, hospitals and emergency settings, helped me to shape my style and ultimately to form the Four Directions System, an approach that continues to grow and evolve as an internationally recognized, unique branch of mindfulness.

Foreword

"All we are is the result of what we have thought."

The Buddha

"Don't believe everything you think. Thoughts are just that—thoughts."

Alan Lokos

My path to knowing Dr. Anthony Stultz and my internal work to "free my mind" originally emanated from what I consider small brushes with mindfulness-based philosophies presented in popular books. Something about what I was reading resonated deeply with me. I kept wondering to myself, "Why haven't I heard of these things before? Why haven't I been taught these concepts in school?"

I was driven to know more. Based on the small exposure to the mindfulness philosophy presented in the books I had read, I researched leading teachers and discovered Tony. That was over 8 years ago.

Since that day, his book has been central to my continuous journey towards awakened thought and clarity of action. I have read it many times over and will continue to do so. Let me share with you just a few examples of what I have learned from this book and how this knowledge has impacted my life.

- Because of my Christian upbringing and western societal norms in general, a part of me was cautious about entering into the world of mindfulness. I have since learned that mindfulness is a psychologically sound philosophy and harmonious with any belief system. The practices are easy to apply and anyone can benefit from these teachings. I think you will find the concepts and philosophies included herein to be both enlightening and practical at the same time.

- As the quote above illuminates, I have learned not to believe everything I think. Our upbringing and societal conditioning is so powerful that our thinking often can be clouded with irrational thoughts. Learning to understand this and recognize when it's happening is critical. But even more importantly, being given the practical tools with which to gain clarity in the midst of the chaotic thoughts is a vitally important life skill. Using these tools in my life has led me to very real changes in my goal setting and vast improvements in my interpersonal relationships with my family and professional colleagues.

- I have also learned that when I am able to get clear with my thoughts, this clarity connects me with my True Self, which is the core of my being and strong enough to handle any situation that comes my way, no matter how painful. Getting to know this inner strength is both comforting and liberating.

- I never before understood the difference between self-esteem and self-confidence. Tony does a masterful job explaining the difference between the two, why both are important, and how your self-esteem cannot be impacted by life's events. At first this seemed counterintuitive to me, but coming to understand this fact is a game-changing mindset. This one concept alone has changed my life in a very profound way.

- Responding to situations rather than reacting has been another invaluable nugget of knowledge. It sounds quite logical and simple, but how many of us truly respond rather than reacting when we are emotionally triggered? Again, Tony provides a practical methodology that enables one to achieve this important goal.

- I have also learned to identify, within myself and among others, which voice is speaking in terms of the communication model of ACR (Archaic/Clear/Reactive). Understanding this model and how it impacts interpersonal communication, and therefore relationships, is paramount to effective interchanges among family members and coworkers. I now understand the importance of utilizing this framework in approaching difficult interpersonal communications. I have since organized training of all my professional staff in how to deploy this model.

- Most importantly, I have learned that the concepts and skills outlined above, in addition to all the other valuable teachings included in this book, are not "once and done" exercises. Tony provides a practical way to begin integrating these concepts and models into daily life, and a way to return to them when you find yourself off-track. Awakening to clarity is a continuous journey and one that requires a practice. I find I am better at practicing at certain times than others, and that's okay. The key is that I know that my new psychological orientation is one that provides for a more grateful and enjoyable life, and it is always there as a guiding light for me to return to. This is why I use this publication as a reference book, returning to its wisdom and guidance when I need to refresh myself and sharpen my skills.

- I have also personally witnessed Tony go into difficult professional and personal scenarios and turn the situations around dramatically, facilitating more authentic and clear relationships while presenting a powerful path towards self-fulfillment. The executive coaching that Tony has provided my companies is unparalleled by anyone we have ever worked with before.

As you can probably tell, the teachings in this book have transformed my personal and professional life. To me, this book is an extremely practical "how to" guide on becoming a creative and compassionate human being, becoming clear in your thinking and about your goals and desires, and improving your interpersonal relationships. Even with all my formal education through a master's level, these are skills I had never learned elsewhere. I will be forever grateful I found them here. I wish you the best on your journey.

Kevin Krause, Principal, American Insurance Administrators and LeadHealth

Introduction

"The greatest weapon against stress is our ability to choose one thought over another"

William James

Before beginning your studies, please consider these ideas:

The title of this book comes from what I believe to be the central message of mindfulness: **freedom**, freedom from unclear thoughts that create painful emotions, unwise actions, and unfortunate consequences. You can be free! In addition, one of the most exciting things about the **Four Directions System of Mindfulness** is that because of the model/exercise approach to the teachings, you can begin to experience positive changes within only a few weeks of starting your practice.

In the chapters that follow I will explain in great detail the application of each direction, but for now I would like to give you an overview of terms that will be very important:

Mindfulness: This is a practice that helps us to understand the thoughts that underlie our emotions and sensations, which in turn underlie our actions. We learn to understand which thoughts are creating unnecessary stress and worry and replace them with thoughts that are clear, helpful and creative.

Meditation: This is a technique that helps to facilitate the mindfulness process by grounding the body in the breath and by the intentional, non-judgmental acceptance of one's emotions, thoughts and sensations occurring in the present moment. While meditation is very useful and can be foundational in the practice of mindfulness, it is not the primary practice. Indeed, one of the reasons our approach has been so successful is that it does not necessarily rely upon daily, seated meditation, which is often not maintained by the individual after the initial training. Our practice, which helps the person restructure cognitively, is easily performed in any setting with immediate results.

The True Self: This term refers to the part of me that is clear and unchanging, no matter what happens in my life. As a metaphor it is the source of my self-respect and self-acceptance, my self-esteem, and my inner ground of peace. Although at trying times in my life I may have difficulty finding the peace and acceptance of my True Self, through the practices of the Four Directions, I know it is always present, always accessible and always complete. This is the source of my clarity, creativity and connection.

The Ego Self: This is a metaphor for my conditioned, reactive self and refers to the part of me that is always changing. It changes and adapts according to the expectations of others, and the expectations that I have learned and placed upon myself. It is the source of self-judgment, whether positive or negative.

The Psyche: This term is synonymous with the concept of the mind as an organic, homeostasis-seeking (or balance-seeking) organism.

Individuation: This is a process of gradual integration and harmonization of the Ego Self through the resolution of successive layers of psychological conflict.

Lucid Clarification: This is the process of practicing mindfulness with specific understanding of the underlying conditioning sources behind our thoughts, feelings and sensations.

<u>The Four Directions System of Mindfulness teaches us to:</u>

STOP! Take time to relax the Ego Self by grounding the body in the breath and by the intentional, non-judgmental acceptance of one's emotions, thoughts and sensations occurring in the present moment.

LOOK! Reorient to the True Self in order to understand life more clearly and compassionately.

LISTEN! Allow the True Self to guide us and free up the uniqueness and creativity of the Ego Self.

As you read each chapter, make sure you take time to *practice the exercises included* and *follow the steps in order*. One of the critical things I have found in using this approach is that it is important to maintain an order while investigating the nature of mind. Try to practice with another person, so that you can clarify the insights you will gain. You can also contact a trained Four Directions System of Mindfulness teacher to work with you:

Mindfullivingtoday.com ~ Dragonflymindfulsolutions@gmail.com

Chapter One
The Five Stages: How the Ego Came to Be

Before we explore the Four Directions, let us look at the basic theory that this method uses to understand how we all develop what we defined earlier as the Ego Self. This theory is called the Principle of Causal or Interdependent Origination. This is important because it will be a very powerful aid in understanding the context for the practices of meditation and mindfulness.

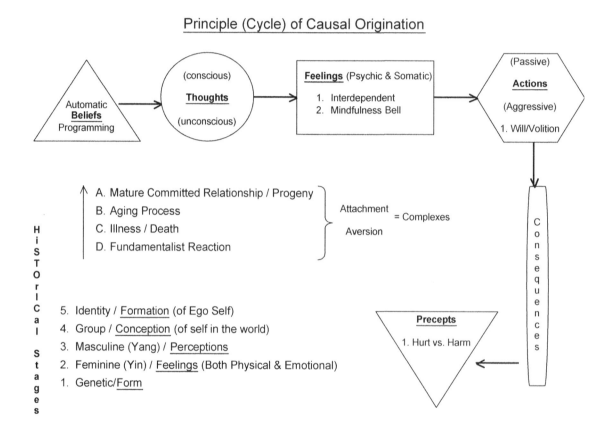

The theory helps us to understand that each person evolves through five stages of development. The events in each stage or aggregate affect or condition us in particular ways.

The first stage is heredity. It includes the genetic material that we inherit from our parents and our other ancestors. This first aggregate is related to the development of our biological form. Much of who we are, from the way we look to the way we act and behave, is heavily influenced by our biological inheritance. It is very important that we understand this, especially if there is any predisposition to disease, or particularly dealing with the psyche, if there is any predisposition to anxiety or depression. This is a very important variable to bring into harmony in achieving our overall goal of wholeness. For example, a person who suffers from manic depression may not experience the full benefit of the Directions without also using a medication.

The second stage is related to the Feeling content (both physical and emotional) of our psyches. This emotional energy is usually created primarily from the relationship we have with our biological mother or the person taking the role of mother in our upbringing. This begins *in utero* and continues all the way through the age of seven or eight. The mother's health and well being while pregnant are included, as are the delivery and any issues such as oxygen deprivation, which could affect the psyche. It also includes the state of the mother's mind, such as if she is depressed or anxious during this period.

The third stage, beginning at the age of eight or nine and lasting through twelve or thirteen, is the Perception stage. It generally refers to our fathers, but I want to emphasize that we are talking about psychic energy so it does not necessarily come from the biological father or even a male. In the case of homosexual parents it could be the person that carries more of the masculine energy in the relationship. This third aggregate in particular seems to be especially vital as individuals develop their perceptions of the outer world (at least at this stage of our species' evolutionary development, where the masculine energy seems to unfortunately dominate both genders) and which function, analytical or intuitive, will dominate those perceptions. People whose fathers were not present or were not emotionally available (or worse, were abusive) during the third phase of growth find that most of their neurotic and troubling tendencies come from this stage.

The fourth stage is the Conception environment that the person has grown up in and is now beginning to explore as an individual. This is the stage where we seek to develop a conception of who we are in the world. This includes social status, philosophy, religion, geographical location, political background and economic status. These become critical at the fourth stage because the person is beginning to explore his or her place in the social system with peers. This stage usually begins around age 13 or 14 and lasts into adulthood, usually reaching completion by age 25 (this may be related to the fact that the brain finishes growing around this same time). For many young adults this stage can produce angst and turmoil as they try to negotiate the tenuous expanse between the powerlessness of being a child and the responsibilities of an adult.

The fifth aggregate, the conscious development of Identity stage, is the final level of development. It begins to emerge in the late third or early fourth stage. *The consciousness development stage is a place where the person develops a very clear or distinct sense of identity* that says: "This is me, this is who I am." As we all know, there is plenty of time in the fourth aggregate when we question who we are and what we will do in life.

Together these five stages or aggregates of conditioning comprise an individual's personality. This is who we *think* we really are, and it is called the Ego Self. To illustrate these concepts more clearly, let us examine an imaginary friend, Joe.

Meet Joe

Joe is forty years old and is a very successful physician. He is married with two young children. He is a pillar of his suburban community and has built a home in the town where he himself spent his boyhood. He has recently taken over his father's medical practice. Joe looks back over his five stages and says to himself, either consciously or most often unconsciously, this is who I am.

If Joe was overly attached to the acceptance of the earlier stages, if he felt he really needed to be (and his parents believed he needed to be), for example, a doctor, then Joe may have become heavily attached to "being a doctor" in order to feel okay. He may have developed what we call an *attachment complex* to that version of his identity. His father was a doctor, and that is the only identity that his parents ever led him to believe was acceptable, so Joe fulfills that. He becomes a physician and moves on into his life.

On the other hand, if he really had difficulty with that early experience and felt alienated by it, he may have developed an *aversion complex* and tried to establish the opposite or the antithesis of those early stages. He pursues his joy in working with engines and becomes an auto mechanic rather than a heart surgeon.

The Psychic Eruptions

What is interesting from the Four Directions perspective is that somewhere along the line, if the person lives long enough, he or she is going to experience one of four events, or eruptions, into the psyche which will cause a sort of reverse or flip-flop of the personality. This, in turn, will lead the person to begin to question the meaning of life.

A) The first event is related to **relationships**. We enter into our very first mature relationship. Usually this involves marriage or a serious commitment. The eruption that leads to questioning may start here. It can also be connected to having a child, which is indeed an even more likely trigger of an eruption.

B) A second potential cause of an eruption is experiencing the process of **aging**. One sees it in oneself or friends or family. These eruptions usually do not happen until later in life when a person begins to experience this kind of change.

C) The third event that can trigger an eruption is experiencing **illness** personally and/or the sickness or **death** of someone close to us. One realizes one's own mortality. This is often so strong or traumatic that it can cause a severe eruption.

D) The fourth eruption is when we reach a **crisis** state and find ourselves in a deep **depression** or with terrible **anxiety**. We then turn to some form of religious or social authority that offers us absolutes that can lift us out of our gloom and satiate our panic.

There is an inherent observation within the Four Directions that our psyche is like an organic system that is always seeking its homeostasis point. This is a point where a system stays in equilibrium as its parts automatically compensate for environmental changes. An eruption and the questioning that flows from it are an opportunity for growth and rediscovering our True Self, which we will discuss further throughout the book.

Anything that we did not work through in our early life, anything with which we did not learn to harmonize, with integrity and awareness, is going to come back at some point because the psyche is seeking homeostasis. The idea is that *the psyche resembles a system that in many ways parallels the universe.* The energy of the psyche transforms in a constant process from simple to complex forms and then returns to simple. It goes through many changes, but the energy is never lost. The mind has a kind of self-correcting mechanism to return to homeostasis, which we call our True Self.

Let us return to Joe. Joe has become a doctor, and he becomes very financially successful. He is married, has children, has a lot of commitments and is a respected member of his community. Then, all of a sudden, seemingly out of nowhere, Joe develops an anxiety about aging and starts to feel trapped by his commitments. He begins to act out in ways that seem very contradictory to his usual personality.

He has likely encountered one of the four experiences that lead to an eruption. What is typical is that Joe will begin to seek distracting excitement and try to recapture aspects of his youth. He might have an affair or suddenly change jobs. We see this all the time, calling it the mid-life crisis. Many people get so caught up in this stage that they make decisions and act in ways that cause divisions that are not reparable.

This is a vital opportunity for a person to find clarity, awareness and self-realization. A person can see situations like this negatively, but from the Four Directions point of view they provide the best opportunities for us to get in tune with what is really going on in our minds.

What about Joe? Joe essentially has developed an aversion complex, the opposite of what his attachment was. He suddenly is going to want to get away from all of the things that he became attached to while growing up that defined him as "okay." He was a respected pillar in the community, but now he is going to care less about that and start focusing on the opposite of all the things that previously defined him. Joe is just going to want what Joe wants (or, at least thinks he wants)!

In many cases, individuals leave their families and their professions abruptly. This is something that is very real and happens to our friends, family members, and even us. We all know examples. It may be that indeed, we need to re-evaluate our relationship or perhaps reconsider our vocational direction. This could lead to the end of a marriage or to a reinvigorated relationship. It could lead to a new career or a renewed approach to our chosen vocation. We all go through these experiences, and they can be very dangerous, like any crisis, *but they are also an opportunity for creativity and transformation.* We can learn to be clear and establish harmony. In the Four Directions we focus on opportunity because simply trying to stop the danger is a dead end. The energy is so strong because there is motivation within the psyche to find wholeness.

Our Basic Programming

How can understanding the five stages and how they relate to our development help us on a daily basis? All of the conditioning of the Ego Self is coalesced into what we might call our "programming system," similar to the operating system of a computer. That basic programming interacts with experiences to create thought patterns, and those thought patterns are hardened into beliefs. Those beliefs in turn create new thoughts, which are based on the same process of conditioning. Those thoughts in turn create feelings, and then behavior follows the feeling. Consequences then flow from behavior.

Programming ~ Thoughts ~ Feelings ~ Actions ~ Consequences

You may not realize it, but you cannot really have a feeling without first having a thought pattern to process; indeed, even the physical reactions of the nervous system are processed by the brain. The trick is that a lot of our thoughts are so automatic and so deeply ingrained that they are unconscious or subconscious. The process from thought to feeling is often so rapid that it seems as if we go right into the feeling mode. We are often unaware of the thoughts that create the feelings and in turn create behavior or actions. The Four Directions practices can help us become aware of this process and enable us to take action, should we choose.

Behavior generally takes one of two forms, passive or aggressive; whether a person chooses one or the other has a lot to do with nature and nurture, the type of personality (introvert or extrovert) as well as the aggregate involved. When one is aggressive in one's behavior, one is *acting* out of the feelings. When one is passive in one's behavior, one is *withdrawing* from a feeling.

These feelings and these actions in turn create consequences. These consequences lead to new thoughts, and the process is reinforced and keeps turning like a wheel. We call this the wheel of *angst*, uncertainty or suffering. That wheel of suffering is perpetuated endlessly not only for the individual Joe or Jodie but for others as it is passed on to friends, associates and especially to one's own children.

Negative conditioning patterns, which begin with one particular person, can be perpetuated for endless generations. The question that can arise at this point is: What can we possibly do about this?

The Process of Individuation

The answer from the Four Directions perspective is that *we can begin to follow the psyche's inherent lure towards wholeness, or the True Self, and we can consciously guide the process.* This is called *individuation.* We can individuate; we can become truly free of the negative conditioning. We can learn how to develop clarity of mind and the ability to understand not only where we come from, but also what we need to do in order to make changes to get the freedom that we so deeply desire. Our personality, which is usually just a conditioned mask or *persona,* becomes transformed into an awakened *person* through whom the True Self can be experienced and creatively expressed.

If we look through the five aggregates, we realize that the feelings which so many people depend on for determining who they are, what they should do, how they should act, or how they should interpret the actions of others are turned upside down by this practice that says you cannot rely on feelings at all. Your feelings are never a good guide for how to act or how to think.

Feelings are understood to be dependent on thoughts for existence; without thoughts they would not exist. We can learn to stop relying on or trusting our feelings to guide us; rather, when we experience a negative feeling we can employ it as a *mindfulness bell,* which is a tool that we can develop through the practices. This metaphorical bell alerts us to the fact that something has hooked us and we need to work at becoming clear. We can then realize that the thoughts themselves are creations of the mind and are not concrete entities.

In terms of actions, behavior is largely about impulse, volition or will. In the beginning of sharing the practices, I do not work much in this area. At times I urge a little bit of intention to get a person motivated, but volition or will alone is not strong enough to completely change us or free us from conditioning. Frankly, people who attempt new goals, whether to lose weight or find a new job, often fail *not because of a lack of will but because of the strength of the unrecognized conditioning.*

In summary, we have plenty of willpower, which relies not on motivation but on a specific focus or concentration; it is our thought processes that sabotage us. However, we can free ourselves from negative thought processes. The will to grow is built into us. It motivates us to begin a practice, even to read this book. When we have difficulty, we can use the practice to get us going again by a conscious act of determination.

The Precepts and Hurt versus Harm

Let us return to the idea of consequences. If we remember the flow diagram, all actions or choices have consequences. In the Four Directions, *precepts* are developed to help a practitioner consider and strategically minimize consequences. I use a version of the precepts at the beginning of each person's practice. The precepts are not commandments; there is no one who is going to punish you if you fall short. They are also not absolute guidelines, but rather generalizations that help us to cut down on consequences.

The first aspect of the precepts can be summed up very simply as, "I will not intentionally cause harm to myself or to another." This is known as *non-harming*; it means that we have a new focus and understanding of the words intention, hurt and responsibility.

Let us look at the two levels of consequences. One level is the mundane level. For example if I take billiard ball A and strike it with billiard ball B, physics and mathematics give me a good idea of what could happen. This is what we call cause and effect. It is a very mundane reality.

However, what we are interested in here is something that is supra mundane, the psychic aspect of cause and effect. Here we learn that the only thing that we really can take responsibility for is our intention, not the outcome.

For example, Joe says something to Betty, and Betty becomes upset and hurt by what Joe says. Joe did not truly intend for it to be hurtful, therefore Joe is not responsible for Betty's feelings. However, one way that he could choose to express his compassion would be to listen deeply to her feelings and possibly relate an experience of his own in which he had been similarly upset. This could possibly open up their relationship to a clearer and more intimate mutuality. However, if he had the intention to cause Betty harm he would have difficulty within his psyche because he is working out of processes that are very negative and destructive. In essence what he is doing is trying to get back at his own negative conditioning by projecting it onto Betty. Projection is an important subject that I will discuss further in chapter three.

Intention is the main consideration, but we also need to understand that there is a great difference between hurt and harm. The reason that I state in the precepts that "I will not intentionally cause harm," is that harm, from the point of view of this practice, is something that requires intention. So if Joe intentionally wants Betty to be upset and he is intentionally causing her harm, then there will be great psychic as well as mundane consequences.

With this realization we can differentiate and begin to *take responsibility for things that we really have some control over, and we can let go of taking responsibility for the things that we do not have control over.* A surgeon who removes a tumor from a person's body has to cause hurt in order to heal by cutting into the body and removing tissue. Maybe radiation or chemotherapy treatments follow that also cause hurt, but the intention of the surgeon is to heal and help.

Again, the first precept is that I will not intentionally cause harm to another person or to myself. Upholding this is going to reduce consequences. Next I add, "…and to help others when I can." I have learned that *intentionally seeking to help others to achieve their fullest potential is the secret to my own fulfillment and happiness as an adult.* However, I cannot really get to the stage of effectively giving help to another until I am much more aware of my intentions. The practices of clarity and awareness found in the Four Directions are a vital foundation.

Summing It Up

An understanding of the way humans evolve and how problems come about is a basic part of the First Direction, which will be discussed in the next chapter. In my work with an individual, we do not spend a lot of time exploring the past; our main concern is the present. However, the past affects our present existence, so we may talk about it a bit with regard to relationships in order to explore the aggregates. Also, some people find that talking about their history or environment can be very helpful in terms of catharsis or release, which can give them a greater sense of motivation. However, according to our framework it will not change a person fundamentally and, in fact, *going into the past too much and stirring up memories without any direction can actually make a person's situation worse.*

We also do not focus on feelings because feelings are so dependent on thoughts for their existence. We are not going to focus on actions other than to engage our willpower or volition, nor will we focus on consequences other than to take the precepts to cut down on negative consequences and try to slow down the wheel of cause and effect.

We are mainly going to learn to focus on our thoughts. First we will do this through meditation in terms of *calm abiding (a period of quiet observation of the thoughts, feelings and sensations that arise in the mind),* and later with mindfulness in terms of *clear seeing (un-obscured insight as to the origins of thoughts, feelings and sensations).* These two methods are the keys to developing awareness. Awareness is our guide throughout the Four Directions.

Chapter Two
The First Direction: Rediscovering the True Self

Our first intention in practice is to step back and take a clearer view of our thoughts and our feelings. We will accomplish this by dividing each Direction into the study of *models,* which are pictorial representations of concepts, and then the application of those models in mental *exercises*. Together, these two modes of practice will allow us to cognitively and experientially grasp the basic ideas of each Direction so that we can apply them in our own lives.

Model One: Self-Esteem and Self-Confidence

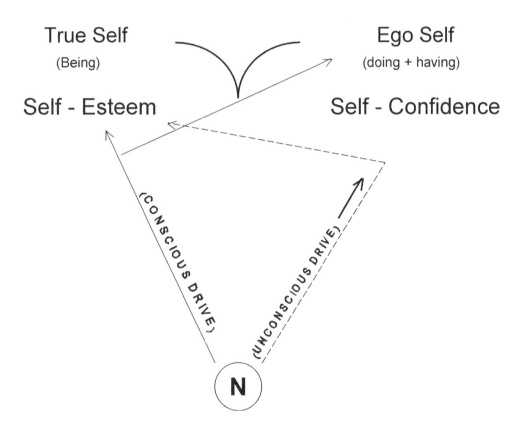

The first model under the First Direction is *the Self-Esteem and Self-Confidence Model*. Most people, when asked, define self-esteem (if they are able to define it at all) as their feelings about themselves or the feelings that others have about them. This reveals an unclear sense of what self-esteem is and where it comes from. To say it is a feeling is incorrect, yet we have all been programmed to believe it. Why?

According to the Four Directions, we evolved from lower life forms into higher life forms. As we did, at some point in our evolutionary history, we became self-conscious creatures and all those survival instincts that brought us to the top of the food chain were integrated into the psyche. We went from being in the realm of the animal world, where we were just unconsciously reacting to our environment, to being self-conscious creatures that could now begin to anticipate things, remember, and use those memories to create situations in the present. That survival instinct as a genome was transferred into the psyche and mutated into a primal aspect of the Ego Self. Consequently, our self-defense mechanisms are now all *about the survival of the ego rather than just the physical body*. It is the same basic defense mechanism except that in beings with highly developed frontal lobes it becomes more complicated and complex. The model of self-esteem that I use asks us to question how we define the term in order to help us redefine it. We will do this in Exercise 1.

Exercise 1: Defining Self Esteem

First, look at the word *esteem,* which is rooted in an economic term that means estimating. When we estimate something we are talking about its value or worth. Everything has a value or worth, but this value or worth depends upon many factors. If I have a bronze plaque that someone I love gave to me and I am asked what its value is, there are many ways to estimate this. I can get it appraised, or I can go on eBay and find out what its market value is. However, to me, because of who it came from and the relationship that it represents to me, its value is likely much, much greater. Our consideration of self-esteem concerns what we believe our inherent value or worth is, and how we come to this estimation.

In order for us to understand this more clearly, I separate this estimation into two categories, self-esteem and self-confidence. These are two worlds that coexist but are not the same. In the Four Directions we call this the relationship between the absolute and the relative. Self-esteem and self-confidence can be seen as two wings of one bird.

In the model we put self-esteem on one side and self-confidence on the other. Self-confidence is the realm of feeling, doing and having; it is the realm of the Ego Self. Self-esteem, however, concerns what we call the True Self, our essential being. The True Self is something inherent and does not depend on what we have or do. The model thus has *being* on the self-esteem side and *doing* and *having* on the self-confidence side.

When people define self-esteem as their feeling about themselves or the feelings that others have about them, this is really in the realm of self-confidence. That is a big surprise to most people! The Four Directions practice takes the radical view that our being is, in essence, of a great inherent value that cannot be determined by self-confidence or the Ego Self side or by doing and having.

Another essential idea is that we are not talking about eliminating one side, but of having both sides together. They are both a part of life. We cannot escape from the experiences of doing and having and we cannot ultimately hide from our experiences in some idealized concept of being.

Exercise 2: Determining the Value of Self Esteem

To help engage both functions of the mind, intuitive and analytical, in understanding this model, I have developed a number system using a scale of 1 to 10.

Much of feeling comes from the intuitive function. Most of our reasoning comes from the analytical function.

Let us say that on the self-esteem side, on a scale of 1 to 10, Joe has an inherent value of 10, which would be the numeric definition of the Ground of his Being. *It is always a 10 no matter what happens in Joe's life.*

The self-confidence side also has a scale of 1 to 10, but a person's estimated level is always going from one extreme to the other. For example, if Joe feels good about himself because he became a doctor like his parents wanted him to be, he might by free association pick his self-confidence level to be around 9. However, if he starts to question that and begins to behave in a way that people do not like, his self-confidence level is going to go down. Likewise, if he is a skilled surgeon and is young and strong, his confidence as a surgeon may be high, a 9, but if he injures his hand or if as he ages his hands become weak or arthritic, his confidence might decrease to a 2.

The realm of self-confidence is insatiable and unstable; it is constantly changing. The numbers for self-confidence are always going from 1 to 10; they are always, like a spiral, going up or down, in constant movement. However, our practice posits the idea that the Being, or self-esteem, side never changes. It is not based on feelings or free association. It is always a 10.

Say that Joe finds a cure for cancer. His self-esteem (being) number stays a 10. It does not go higher. On the other hand, if this same cure turns out later to have unfortunate and deadly side effects, his number on the self-confidence (doing and having) side is going to naturally go down. However, and this is the main point, his self-esteem (being) side will remain the same. *His Being stays a 10*, and this allows him a constant ground from which to start over again.

Next, let us imagine that we all are born with an inner compass that aids us in an orientation and sets up a proverbial mental north. Because of the way that we have evolved, our inner compass points first to doing and having to try to achieve and maintain a sense of being. This has a many-fold effect, but two insights that arise are especially relevant. One is that anything that we do begins, in our perception, to carry the weight of our entire being with it. Yet nothing we can do, no relationship, job, status or talent can really carry the weight of our Being. That is why those things fail to ultimately satisfy us, why people who have material possessions, good looks, success and status can be just as depressed, just as anxious and just as disturbed as anybody else.

The second insight is that if we want to make changes to improve self-confidence but are always unconsciously trying to improve our worth, we often fail to see the actual changes that we need to make to improve our performance. For example, I love to tell folks about an interview I once read about Thomas Edison after he had created the first commercial light bulb. The interviewer observed that the quest to find a commercial bulb had required 5000 different experiments. He then asked Edison what it was like to fail 4,999 times. Edison, taken aback, said that he had honestly never looked at it that way. To him it was just a 5,000-step process.

Unfortunately, we tend to do the opposite and adopt a less objective point of view and may consider any mistakes we make to be fatal. Therefore we either ignore character flaws and continue to make the same errors that we have always tended to make, or we retreat into the false safety of not attempting anything that would truly challenge us and help us to grow.

What we want to do in our new approach is to shift the focus. We are not trying to get rid of the Ego Self. This is a vitally important point. A lot of philosophies and religions talk about the Ego Self as some terrible, negative thing, and if we can only rid ourselves of our egos, then we will be okay. Frankly, the only people that I have ever met that had no Ego Self were clinically psychotic.

From a practice point of view, this understanding of the Ego Self/True Self dynamic ultimately leads us beyond an either/or dichotomy. The absolute participates in the relative, the relative in the absolute. The True Self and Ego Self are interdependent. What we are talking about is a change of orientation, a change in direction. We are putting the Ego Self into its proper normal harmonious and holistic perspective. We enable the shift by *establishing the True North of our inner compass as the True Self.*

By changing that orientation, by going to the True Self for our understanding of Being first, and then to the self-confidence world, two things happen. First of all *we can find happiness and wellness and then pursue individual goals*. This is very different from the belief that if we achieve individual goals first, then we will be happy. We turn the whole thing upside down! For example, many people have studied the psychologist Abraham Maslow and his pyramid called the hierarchy of needs. At the top of that pyramid is self-actualization. The ideal person has to have the right shelter, education, status, etc. before achieving or being concerned with self-actualization. In the Western world, unfortunately, if you are lucky, if you are male, white and European, you may get to that point; if you are anything else, your chances are reduced.

The self-esteem model takes that pyramid and flips it upside down by teaching that you can experience a state of self-actualization first and then all those other things (doing and having) can actually become manifestations of the True Self. The Four Directions offers people this fantastic notion. That is why it is so appealing and so many people have found this approach to be very useful. It cuts across gender and cultural heritage, and goes beyond all the dictates of the genome of survival.

A very easy way to look at this is to imagine a young child is placed on your doorstep, and you have to take responsibility to raise him or her. You can choose either one of those orientations for that child. You can say, "You know what, Joe? Right now you're 10 but let's see how you do as you grow, let's see how good-looking you are, let's see how much intelligence and talent you have, where you come from, what kind of family you have and the color of your skin." Then all these things begin to create Joe's identity. He may become a 9 or he may be a 1, it all depends on what he is given.

Or you can say, "Joe, you are a 1 right now, but if you work really hard, if you do all the right things, you might get to be a 9, but don't screw up or make any mistakes. Make sure you get all A's."

Or you can nurture Joe by saying, "Joe, you, by being born, have an inherent worth of self-esteem, and it is a 10. That's as high as it can get. It will never go lower, and it is always the place to which you can return, no matter what you do or have. You will always be a 10."

Which orientation do think is more likely to lead Joe to grow up into an adult who is generally happy, has a sense of well-being and sees life as an adventure, and when he has problems, can find positive, creative ways to deal with them? It is obvious. Anybody who is shown this model, whether they are corporate executives or teenagers, can see the benefit of the self-esteem orientation.

Again, that is not how we usually do things; that is not how we have been raised. Why is that? It is because we are largely unconscious or not awake. We have, by our primitive conditioning, been programmed like robots or puppets to, at all expense, survive and get to the top of the heap. This unfortunately creates an egocentric, selfish person.

The truth is that we do not have to live like this. It is a paradox that self-consciousness not only brought all this about in terms of the psyche, but it is *through this same ordinary mind that we can find freedom and liberation and have real, lasting happiness.* We can choose to live from the Self-Esteem Model.

Model Two: Wholeness versus Perfection

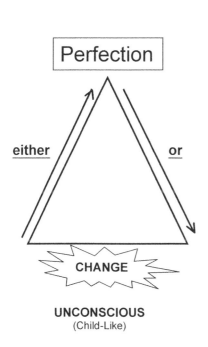

"Ego Self Triangle"

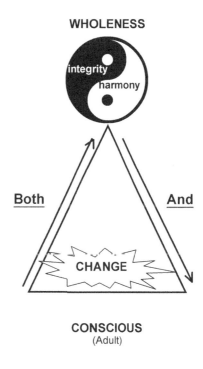

"True Self Triangle"

This model has two pyramids or triangles. Again, one triangle is based on the Ego Self and the other triangle is based on the True Self. The Ego Self side has a triangle with a square at the top. In that square is the word "perfection." Going up each side of the triangle is an arrow pointing towards the square, showing that perfection is the goal. The orientation of the Ego Self is an unconscious attempt to try to achieve the Square of Perfection.

From the Four Directions point of view, that square is a delusion. It never existed, and it never will exist. There is terrible fallout from pursuing perfection. The fallout is that we begin to see the world in terms of either/or, black and white. We are seeking perfection, and we believe that it exists. However, I challenge people to tell me anything in this world that is perfect. Most of us have been conditioned to look at the world as an either/or reality, black or white, perfect or imperfect. This view or attitude is a delusion that distorts how we look at life and how we deal with life experiences.

Outside of the Ego Self triangle is the word "change" with all kinds of danger zigzags surrounding it. Change becomes the enemy because we are either trying to get change so that we gain some sense of perfection or trying to avoid change to prevent the loss of the perfection that we think we have achieved.

The reason that we need a new model is that often we try to get rid of an old model when it is negative or not working for us, but then we do not replace it with anything else. Thus, there is no foundation or model for the psyche to use. When it gets into trouble it uses whatever model is available. We have all had this perfection model for a long time. It has evolved for untold millennia. We cannot pretend that the solution is just to get rid of it; science tells us that nature abhors a vacuum, and this is just as true for the psyche as it is for the universe. We will replace this perfection model with the wholeness model.

The wholeness model is based on the True Self. We still try to pursue things. That is the way we are made. Change is no longer outside of the triangle of our life, but has now been integrated. It is no longer the enemy; it is opportunity, the opportunity to be creative and do something new. The goal at the top of the True Self triangle is different from the Ego Self triangle, and I put a circle around it rather than a square.

The circle represents a home for our new goal of wholeness, or becoming whole. We all inherently know we are drawn to wholeness. In the circle is a yin-yang symbol. One part is integrity and the other part is harmony.

Integrity here is not referring to a moral position, but rather it means that I can integrate everything in my life: the good, the bad and the ugly. I can integrate all of it into one. Every part has a place. I do not push any of the difficult or dark stuff away. I do not have a Pollyanna-like view; I see reality as it is, and I can integrate all of my experiences. This process is about clarity, not about any particular philosophy of negativism or positivism, pessimism or optimism. There is the *paradoxical riddle* of a glass that is half empty to a pessimist and half full to an optimist, but our practice says that it is just a glass of water, <u>so drink</u>. Because our practice is about clarity, we can choose what we want to emphasize. We decide whether the universe is for or against us.

It is also about empowerment. It empowers us to choose freedom. *We are free to choose, and we can make decisions about who we are and what our reality is.* I can create my life in any way I wish. My life becomes my art. A radical idea!

The other side, harmony, means you can find a way to establish harmony in all aspects of your life and integrate those aspects in a way that is well-balanced and fosters a view of life as a creative gift. The pursuit of this goal leads to a both/and attitude, instead of either/or, black or white. The world becomes, as it is, both this *and* that. The world can be beautiful and wonderful and also very ugly and terrible. People can be thoughtful and compassionate and they can be very horrible and destructive, too. The reality is both.

Exercise 3: Reorientation Meditation

The next exercise is called Reorientation Meditation and it will help us to establish the True North of our inner compass as the True Self. We will do this through a very powerful, successful and subtle technique. When we are growing up through the five aggregates, most of our conditioning takes place in a pre-cognitive, pre-contextual manner, before a fully developed ego identity forms. In reorientation I use many of the insights from innovative educators such as Jean Piaget and Maria Montessori. We see the developing being as a sponge. Material is absorbed on a sub-cognitive (subconscious) level, a sensory level.

To start our re-orientation, we create and establish *a centering space,* which is an actual physical space.

The Centering Space

A. Centering Object

B. Stand or Altar

C. Incense and Incense Bowl

D. Candle

E. Flower with Vase

F. Water Bowl

G. Bell

In your centering space you will place certain elements. In the center is an object that, to you, represents wholeness. It can be anything, but it must personally resonate with you. I like to use circular shapes because I believe that circles are nature's inherent way of pointing us to wholeness. This central object represents the True Self.

On the right side, put a candle that can be lit and extinguished. The candle represents that this is not a one-time thing. This is a practice that you choose to do every day. You cannot just do it once and then forget about it. Change comes through osmosis; it is a process that requires a daily return. The flame itself symbolizes to us the light of enlightenment.

On the left, put a flower in a vase. The life cycle of the flower is a natural process and communicates to us in a visual way that everything is beautiful and everything is impermanent and goes through changes. As the flower wilts and dies, we know its beauty is passing; we replace it with a new one.

Also, put out a bowl of water; water is a very powerful symbol of healing, purity and clarity. We all can imagine the still calm of a pond or things flowing like water. Water is 90 percent of what we are all made of; it is the very essence of our life force in terms of the material world.

Next, use a bell of some sort, which reminds us of and calls us to wholeness, the basis of the True Self. It is the voice of our True Self calling the Ego Self home.

I also recommend the use of incense that we light from the candle. The incense is a metaphor for our daily practice. We allow its fragrance and essence to permeate our most primal sense, our sense of smell. It represents our 'giving back' to the universe in a mindful way, leaving the perfume of an examined life that is lived freely and fully. Long after we are gone from the stage of this drama, the way in which we lived our life will continue in the environment of the lives that we have touched.

Lastly, we bring our body into it by putting our hands together, bowing, and saying to ourselves, "I take refuge in my True Self." We will say that each day, morning and evening.

By doing just these physical actions, we tap into the primal aggregates. However, this time, instead of someone conditioning us, we are doing it ourselves; we are finally in charge of our own destiny.

When you get up in the morning, the first thing to do, at the very least, is bow in the direction of that space. See it, take it in, and then go on your way to shower, brush your teeth or whatever. But do that first upon waking. At night, after you read, watch a movie or make love, but before you go to sleep, take refuge in the knowledge that this is the Ground of your Being. This is the Source of all wisdom, compassion and happiness. Whatever happened that day, this is still your true Source. Some people ask me if it is necessary to do this practice everyday, and I suggest that they only do it as often as they practice physical hygiene and that they consider this a form of mental hygiene. Most people find it useful to at least light the candle and the incense and ring the bell. Do whatever you feel is necessary. Experiment and find what works best for you.

In addition, take time throughout the day or mark the beginning and the end of the cycle of the day by going back and returning to the teachings. Take at least 10 to 20 minutes to contemplate the models and go over them. Contemplate constantly so you know the models by heart.

Test the models within your experience, because the most important thing about this practice is finding what works for you. I suggest that you keep a journal and use a number system to evaluate yourself. Every day at the beginning or the end, it doesn't matter which, give yourself a number from 1 to 10 describing how you are feeling and really try to use the first number that pops into your head. This is called free association in psychology and it helps to bypass the ego's defenses a little bit. This is typically what we do in dreams, daydreams and fantasies. This number provides a way for you to track the progress of your moods as you practice and also helps to alert you to circumstances that tend to ignite uncomfortable feelings coming from unclear thoughts that need to be clarified. Writing these things down or talking about them changes the way the brain processes them. It really allows us to look at things in a whole new way.

Using this approach allows us to begin to see that our feelings are changing, and what is changing our feelings is not our environmental situation, it is not our past, it is not our future. *What is changing is the way we think.*

Exercise 4: Relaxation Meditation

In this exercise we want to develop a way to allow the Ego Self to deeply relax. This can be accomplished through almost any activity that a person finds relaxing mentally and physically, but the two that we recommend the most are *sauntering and sitting still*.

Sauntering practice just involves taking a walk for ten to twenty minutes a day, with no goal or destination. That's it!

Sitting practice involves taking time to find a comfortable place to sit quietly and either recite the mantra, "I take refuge in my True Self," (alternatively, you may wish to use a more traditional word-sound like "Om," which is used in yoga) or pay attention to the body breathing. We can also use an object that we can run through our fingers (we recommend a mala, or meditation beads) or an object that we fix our gaze upon, like a spot on a wall or our centering space.

While we are sitting (for 10 to 20 minutes), whenever a thought, feeling or physical sensation arises, we just acknowledge it briefly, take a deep breath and continue. The point of this exercise is to not push our thoughts, feelings and sensations away, but also not to go into them. One method that seems to be helpful is to imagine your thoughts, feelings and sensations as clouds passing through the open and spacious sky of your awareness. Some are dark and filled with rain and some are white and filled with light, but the point is that *they pass.*

Another method is to sit quietly and listen to the sounds all around you. As you experience the sounds, you realize that they can affect your emotional state. A loud bang can make you feel anxious or a soft hum can make you feel relaxed. You do not usually identify with the sound itself; rather you recognize that it is an object of your senses. However, when it comes to thoughts, we tend to associate them as subjects, as less objective. We accept the delusion that our thoughts are who we are.

By doing this practice daily, we begin to allow our Ego Self to relax into the embrace of our True Self, which is always serene and peaceful. This practice will gently prepare us to begin making inquiries into the nature of our Ego Self conditioning, which we will learn about in chapter three.

Chapter Three
The Second Direction: Understanding the Ego Self

Our next model, the *Archaic /Clear/Reactive Model,* is very familiar in Western psychology. It focuses on different states of the Ego Self. In this chapter we are going to delve deeper into a proposed structure of the psyche. In the following models and exercises we will learn to analyze our mind patterns so that we may gain an inner locus of control and communication.

There are three ego states, traditionally called the parent, the adult and the child. In this practice, the first state, the parent or archaic, does not necessarily just represent our biological parents but represents the whole five-stage historical development. We use the word parent to recognize that this is the old stuff, the original conditioning, the archaic programming.

Again we realize that *there is a yin and yang to everything.* The parent conditioning has two faces. One side of the parent, the yin side, is nurturing. It is very creative, positive and loving. The other side, yang, is the critical and destructive aspect of the parent.

In turn, this creates an inner child/reactive aspect with two faces, or two parts. The key to understanding the child is that it is the realm of the affective (emotional) and somatic (physical) expression of our Being. The first part of the child is what we call the natural child. The natural child is the aspect that naturally flowers or grows under the nurturing of the parent. There are certain demarcations or earmarks of the natural child. One is a sense of happiness, freedom and well being, an inherent sense of, "I am okay." There is a personal comfort with one's sexuality and a general sense of physical health and vigor. There is also a strong sense of humor.

In turn, the other side of the parent, the destructive or critical side, creates in us the adapted child, the child that had to adapt to all the negative criticism and conditioning. The earmarks of that aspect are generally those of someone who is not well. Mentally he or she is often depressed or very anxious. Physically there is often a lot of sickness or illness, a lack of vigor or vitality. In the adaptive child, instead of a sense of humor, there is often sarcasm. In sexual expression, there is either frigidity or promiscuity. *The adaptive child, or hurt child, creates a wall of defense mechanisms around itself to try to survive the criticism and the negativity of the parent.*

The parent represents all the aggregate stages, even the social and the biological. This circle of protection around us is maintained by the defense mechanisms. We create these defense mechanisms as an unconscious way to survive, but the problem is that a child created them, the archaic and innocent child.

This primitive child in us is not only related to our primitive evolutionary beginning as an individual, but also to our entire evolutionary history as a species. Fight and flight responses are related to it, as this defense mechanism usually takes on one of these two aspects with regard to reaction. Remember the model of the five stages and the discussion about will or volition? In this case, if we choose to fight, we try to strike out at the critical parent. The ultimate example of striking out against that negative conditioning is homicide. What I discovered when working in prisons is that many people who engage in violent behavior are really trying to attack that conditioning. If we choose the 'flight' mode, we begin to withdraw or dissociate from the critical parent. The ultimate expression of this is when the person tries to destroy him- or herself with either a slow (addiction) or immediate suicide. The person projects this negativity onto something else because his or her need for acceptance by the object of the projection (the parent) is too great.

The PAC (Archaic/Clear/Reactive) Model

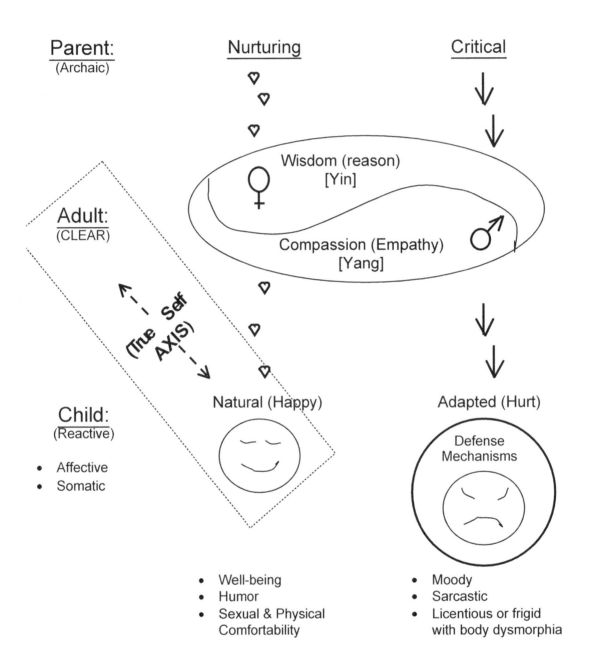

Exercise 5: Finding the Adult

Let us return now to our character Joe, and let's say Joe's father used to beat him or that Joe was sexually molested. Joe will often then act out towards another person onto whom he projects that energy, but what he is really trying to do is to reconcile with the aggression and fear that he felt at the hands of his father.

If he found the sexual experience to be pleasurable, but as a prepubescent child he had no mature, cognitive context or conceptuality, then he may as a young adult become promiscuous. If he found the experience disturbing, then as a young adult he will probably withdraw from physical contact and be very confused about his sexuality.

The other extreme, passive action or behavior, is to try to do things to gain the sympathy and attention of the parent and to try to revert back to a dependent state. This is where we see a lot of drug addiction and other addictive behaviors. The ultimate experience of trying to escape the parent is suicide. That is how powerful this relationship conditioning is.

In the middle we have our saving grace, our conduit from the Ego Self to the True Self, and that is what we call the adult/clear aspect. The adult is the intermediary between the parent and the child. It represents a person who is awake. The adult also has two parts, a yang and yin aspect. The yang aspect is compassion. The adult in us knows how to be empathetic; it knows how to be compassionate. Secondly, the adult in us knows how to reason because it has wisdom, the yin aspect.

Model Three: The Captain's Chair or Psychic Feng Shui

One of the things that we do in the mindfulness approach is to give ourselves time for the adult to come on board as we meditate and reorient ourselves. In the model of the psyche that I use, I put a captain's chair in the center of a circle representing the psyche. For most people the parent is sitting in the captain's chair, and underneath the chair is the adapted child, while behind the chair, every now and then, poking its head out, is the adult.

(PAC) Captain's Chair Model

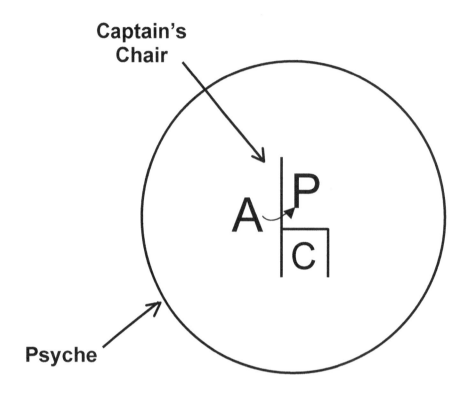

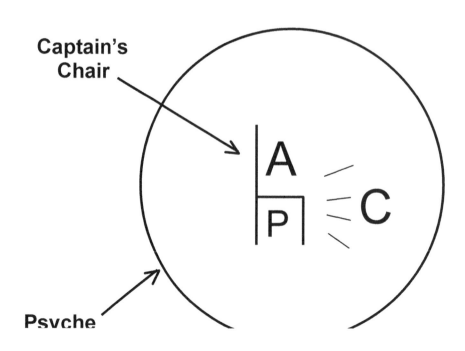

We now want to create a new model. Our new model is the adult sitting in the captain's chair of the psyche, the critical parent is put under the chair, and the natural child is set free but under the protection and supervision of the adult.

It is wise to differentiate the aspects, but once more we are not getting rid of anything. We are integrating everything while just changing orientation. It is like the psychic application of the Chinese idea of *Feng-Shui*, or finding harmonious placement.

How does this work? The meditation exercises that we learned earlier give the adult time to come aboard and get into the chair. *The first thing that the adult offers is compassion towards our own inner child, because that child is not going to be set free until it feels loved and safe. We can do this for ourselves.* We can become our own best friend and our own best companion by first and always offering compassion to that hurt part of us. When the child in us feels safe, then we can offer wisdom and reason. However, if we try to reason without allowing it to express itself, without allowing it to be known, our efforts will be in vain.

Labeling and Observing

A. Thoughts

B. Emotions

C. Sensations

D. Awareness

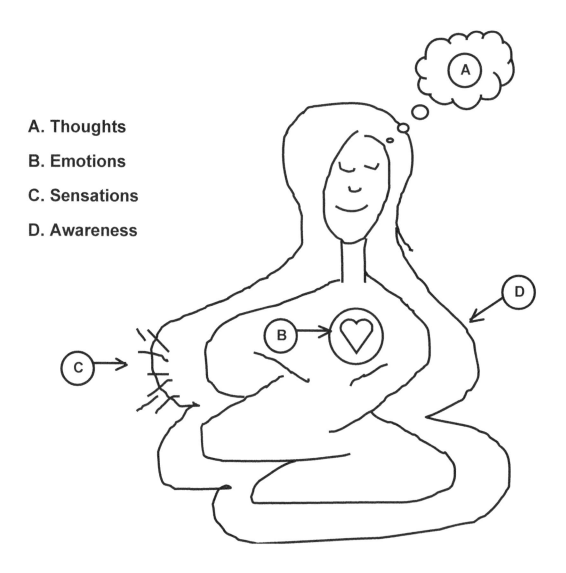

Exercise 6: Labeling and Observing

The Parent/Adult/Child Model offers us a new language that I often use in relationship work. With Exercise 3 we began to see what practicing sitting meditation can give us. Now, while we are meditating and observing our thoughts, we add the process of labeling where a thought or feeling is coming from so we can see whether its source is the parent, adult or child.

We begin this labeling practice with sitting meditation, and it is very simple. Find a time during the day where you can sit for least 10 minutes, but for no more than 20 minutes. Usually you can do this combined with one of your periods of Reorientation practice. While sitting I want you to simply use your breath. Watch or count each breath from 1 up to 10, then start with 1 again. You can also use a repetitive word or mantra that you have been using in Reorientation. Then basically let your mind do what it does. You have to sit quietly in order to give yourself a chance to listen, which is an important part of this practice. Sometimes you may be a little agitated, and then it is good to saunter (walk) or do some moving meditation (tai chi, yoga, etc.) first before you sit.

When a good thought arises, you do not want to become too attached to it. You also do not want to develop any aversions if an unpleasant thought comes into your mind. You just want to let the thought be and then to go back to focusing on the breath. If a pleasant or unpleasant physical sensation arises, again you do not want to be too attached to or averted from it.

You want to develop a strong sense of acceptance during your sitting. Maybe a feeling comes up that is really strong. Remember, just let it pass, neither holding on to it nor rejecting it. The point is that you want to accept all that you feel. If you are being drawn in or being pushed away by a thought or a feeling or a sensation, you simply want to return to your breathing to stabilize yourself and bring yourself back to the present moment. Those thoughts and feelings will try to drag you back into the past or push you ahead into the future. By learning to identify with your awareness you can learn to live more in the present moment, or what some call the "eternal now".

The next part of this practice is when a thought comes up, you can simply label it as a thought, "I'm having a thought." When you feel something, say to yourself, "I'm having a feeling." If it is a physical sensation you say, "I'm having a physical sensation." The purpose here is to recognize that you are starting to associate with your awareness rather than those thoughts or feelings, and you are starting to use a different language. You are not sad; you are feeling sad. You are not depressed; you are feeling depressed. You are simply being, not doing and having.

As you start to get more comfortable with this, you can begin to look at the process in terms of the parent, adult and child. You can say, "I'm having a thought that is coming from the parent," or "I'm having a feeling that's coming from the hurt child." Then go back to the breath.

For example, you are sitting there and suddenly you think, "That person really does not like me, but I should not think that way." You have just had two thoughts. Using the model, you realize that the first thought, that the person really does not like you, is coming from the hurt child. The second thought, that you should not be thinking that way, is coming from the critical parent. You can also use a time reference and say that it is coming from the past or the future. The adult is always in the now, in the present.

It is a very simple and easy practice, but it does take effort and repetition. Soon you can train yourself to think with clarity and be able to stay focused and present. What we are engaged in is discipline, which simply means self-guidance. This differs from a habit, as a habit is a combination of conditioning and exposure. For example, no child has to learn to like sugar. One try and he or she is hooked for life. This is because our ancient ancestors discovered sugar in fruits, and a strong reaction to it is now built into us. However, learning to balance one's consumption of sugar is a demonstration of discipline.

Exercise 7: The Psychic Disarm or Mental Ju-Jitsu

Up until now, we have been learning how to respond to our own internal thoughts, feelings, and sensations. Exercise 7 takes us out of ourselves a bit and helps us to respond to negative feelings coming from our interactions with another person. When someone is attacking you psychologically or you want to overcome an individual's defense mechanism, these three simple steps will allow you to compassionately disarm the person (or persons) and redirect the situation to create better communication and connection. The reason I call it Mental Ju-Jitsu is because I am a self-defense teacher as well, and in our form of martial art we teach folks that the best defense is to not become a target and to redirect the attacker's force.

1. *Acknowledge* that your own defense system has been affected and let the thoughts and feelings arise and wash over you by taking deep breaths (just like in meditation).

2. *Employ* the Disarm by finding something to agree with in what they are presenting, even if you don't completely agree or it is only 1% out of 100% (you could also just politely dismiss yourself and walk away, but this would not be as effective). You will know you have successfully accomplished the Disarm when the person does not know what to say or seems confused and unable to react. You have taken yourself out of the equation and are no longer a target.

3. *Redirect* the person(s) by connecting compassionately with the hurt child aspect of the Ego Self and move on to a place of clarity. Try not to fill up the silence with too many words. One of the interesting phenomena we have found is that folks at this juncture will often come up with a good solution to the issue at hand without you having to say anything.

Here is an example:

I was once giving a seminar to a large group at a university on the subject of anger. Right after I was introduced, a large man in the back of the auditorium stood up and went to one of the microphone stands that had been set up in the aisle for the question and answer portion of the talk. He interrupted my introduction and said, "I think that all of this stuff is just psycho mumbo-jumbo and a waste of my time!" The crowd turned to look at him and then back at me. It was one of those, "teachable moments." I took several slow deep breaths and let the thoughts arising roll over me (Step 1), thoughts like, "What an idiot! I should go over there and stick that microphone where the sun doesn't shine!" and "I have more intelligence in my finger than that guy has in his whole body!" This took a few seconds. I could now choose to ignore him or employ the Disarm. I chose the latter by softly and sincerely saying, "You know, what you say is true. A lot of the pop psychological stuff out there is just mumbo-jumbo. And in fact what I will show you will only probably work about 75% of the time."(Step 2) He didn't know what hit him! Everyone in the audience turned toward him. Silence. I then said, "But you good folks have paid me to share what I know so that I might be helpful in some way. Once I have finished, please absorb what is useful and let go of what isn't. And sir, please see me afterward as I would really like to answer any questions that you may have." (Step 3) With that, the man sheepishly went back to his seat and I continued my presentation. After it was over, I noticed that he was waiting for me. I politely excused myself and went over to shake his hand. We sat down and he proceeded to tell me how his troubled younger brother had gone to a counselor for help but still ended up committing suicide. This man was projecting on to me the counselor that he imagined had let his brother down. We chatted for a bit and then I invited him to talk with me more at another time. He would do so, traveling to my office regularly for the next three months.

Exercise 8: Externalizing the Psychic Dialog

This exercise includes two techniques. They both require a facilitator who is familiar with the Four Directions process. In technique one, we sit two people in front of one other and have one person play his or her own Ego Self voice while the facilitator plays the voice of the other person's True Self. It is important that we remember that the True Self always begins with compassion and then moves into wisdom. When the Ego Self voice gets stuck or can't respond, the True Self begins to guide it towards clarity.

Here is a verbatim example:

> *Ego Self: You're an idiot and a loser. You'll never be happy.*
> *True Self: Please tell me more.*
> *ES: What more do you need? You just don't count!*
> *TS: That is exactly how I feel.*
> *ES: Who cares what you feel?*
> *TS: I do.*
> *ES: Why do you care?*
> *TS. I'm not sure. What do you think?*
> *(At this point the Ego Self voice faltered and began to search for a response.)*
> *TS: Please, I really do want to know.*
> *ES: (Begins to let down its defenses and speak of its pain.)*

In this little transaction the True Self employed our Psychic Ju-Jitsu; in other words, it disarmed the Ego Self not by protecting itself, but by becoming "empty" or transparent so that the Ego Self had nowhere to go but to open up and speak its pain. You will notice that the Ego Self initially began by using a parental tone and then when it got stuck it began to use the hurt child tone.

The second technique is much simpler and less sophisticated, just requiring the facilitator to ask to speak first to the parent and then to the child. It is important to follow in this order as the Ego Self uses the parent tone to protect the child.

Here is another example:

> *True Self: You are a strong protector, may I have your permission to speak to the Hurt Child?*
> *Ego Self: What for? Who are you anyway?*
> *TS: I mean you no harm. I only want to listen.*
> *ES: Why?*
> *TS: Why not?*
> *ES: Okay, but if I suspect anything negative the interview is over!*
> *TS: Yes, of course. Am I speaking to the Hurt Child?*
> *ES: Yes.*
> *TS: How are you feeling?*
> *ES: Afraid.*
> *TS: I am afraid sometimes too. What are you afraid of?*

At this point the True Self tries to discover a specific strong feeling and then query as to the strong thought that created it in the first place. This is a more advanced technique that you will learn later on in this book.

Transpersonal Model of the Psyche

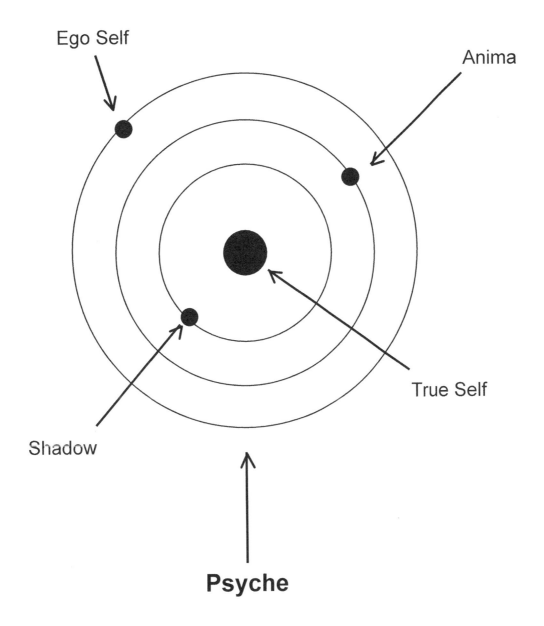

Model Four: The Transpersonal Model

The next model that I use comes from a *transpersonal or "beyond persona"* view of the self. Some of the language is taken directly from depth psychology, much in the same way that I took some of the language from transactional psychology (model of the parent, adult and child) to transliterate the ancient mindfulness insights. This model helps us to more deeply understand the power of *Projection.*

The transpersonal model is somewhat like a solar system model of the psyche. Draw a big circle. In the solar system this would be the sun, but in this model we label the center circle True Self. Draw a concentric circle outside of that, and label it the Shadow. Draw another concentric circle and label it the Anima. Draw one more concentric circle, which is at the outer edges of the psychic solar system, and label it the Ego.

This practice is really about reorientation, just as we talked about at the beginning of the book. When the Ego considers itself to be the center, it looks out beyond its own psychic solar system for meaning rather than looking within to understand and interpret events that are occurring. It looks outside into the world of objects to try to interpret and find meaning. The Ego Self, because of its evolutionary orientation, thinks it is about the world of doing and having. The inner world of the True Self, because of its timeless nature, knows it is about the world of Being.

The circle that is closest to the Ego is the Anima, a Latin word that means spirit. The Anima is that part of us that represents our creative energy and sometimes is referred to as libido energy or sexual energy, but it really does not refer to that alone. It also refers to the creative things that excite and animate us. The Anima is a conduit to the True Self. What really turn us on and drives our creativity can be a way for us to connect to our True Self.

The circle closest to the True Self is the Shadow. The Shadow is made up of all the material that gets displaced by the defense mechanisms of our hurt child, the repressed material our hurt child does not want or know how to deal with. This energy has to go somewhere; the Four Directions views the psyche as a closed and growing universe that retains everything. The Shadow gets all of that material.

Why is the Shadow so close to the True Self? *Most of the information that is revealed in the Shadow and brought out in the light of mindfulness is what most quickly gets us into harmony with our True Self.* We have been hiding from this secret treasure, afraid to use it and see it for what it is. The Anima is the stuff that is usually much more fun for us to deal with, and it is the Shadow material that we tend to be afraid of because we interpret it literally rather than symbolically. The Shadow material should be taken as a metaphor.

For example, Sue thinks, "I hate this person, I wish he were dead." That is a child's thought. Then Sue begins to say, "I shouldn't have those feelings." This is a parental thought. Next Sue begins to think that she is not a good person (being), even though in reality she really does not wish that person to be dead. She just wishes the situation would go away.

Suicidal ideation is based on the same process. For example, a person who is depressed may have suicidal thoughts, which in itself may not be dangerous. In fact these thoughts would not really indicate a desire for death, but rather a way to escape problems. From an awakened point of view, suicidal thoughts may indicate metaphorically the need for an old and fixated ego identity to change or 'die' and be reborn as a fresh and more flexible sense of self.

With mindfulness you can start to realize that most of the information that comes from the Shadow is metaphorical. Then you will not be afraid of it anymore; you can open up and be receptive to it. Most people are afraid to do this because they do not want to see the ugly or the bad in themselves even though that often is what is pushing their buttons. The Shadow can turn into a very rich resource of clarity and understanding for reuniting with the True Self.

For Sue this means that she could express empathy for the hurt child within her, without allowing it to dictate her emotions or behavior. It would also mean that she could accept her negative 'should' thought as an awkward and unhelpful attempt at asking her to look at the situation differently. Parental admonitions often are just initial inappropriately authoritative voices that while intending to help us, only reinforce our negative conditioning.

The Anima is most often experienced when a person is not awakened and not turning inward to the True Self. He or she projects that energy onto a person, place or thing. For example, by saying, "Boy, if I only had this person in my life or this thing or this situation, then I'd be happy," this person projects his or her energy outwards rather than focusing it inwards to discover what he or she needs to do creatively. This is called transference. *Transference* occurs from the ego to the person, place or thing. In psychology transference is the process whereby a person unconsciously redirects feelings or emotions onto another person, place or thing and that object sends information back, which is called *counter-transference*.

It is the process by which the traumas and dramas of old relationships are re-experienced in new ones. I see a lot of this in counseling. Not only do we project individually, we also do so collectively. After 9/11 it became very easy for us collectively to project our Shadows onto people of Arab descent or people of the Muslim faith. Transference is very easy to do. What we really need to do is find out from the Shadow what it is trying to communicate to us.

Joe and Betty

Let us say Joe is having difficulties with his girlfriend, Betty. He meets a new girl and suddenly feels that he needs to be with this new girl and that he would be much happier with her than he is with Betty. When he thinks about this new girl he gets excited, and all these new pleasant thoughts arise. In reality he has projected his Anima onto this new girl. At one time he did that with Betty, but after a while, projections were all that were left because the relationship did not evolve to help Joe see and appreciate that Betty is a real person, not just a projection.

Every relationship involves projection and transference. The best relationships, according to the Four Directions, involve a person who is aware of the fact that he or she is nearly always projecting. Then one can truly decide to love and appreciate the other person without overvaluing or objectifying him or her, without expecting another to carry one's whole psychic Anima.

It is very unfair for Joe to use this new projection to make any decisions about his relationship with Betty because there is no way Betty can carry his projection. Nobody can do that for Joe; he must do it for himself. Maybe Joe then comes to someone like me, a counselor. The first thing I would say is, "Joe, we realize this new girl is a projection of your Anima. What this situation is trying to say to you is to turn inward, there's something you need to create, there's something you need to look at that you are ignoring. Whether or not your relationship with Betty is something you need to change or re-evaluate is another question. Before you can get to that, you have to recognize what is really happening and ask yourself what the new situation is trying to teach you."

Exercise 9: Imagination Meditation

This is where the practice of imagination meditation comes in. I may say to a person, "Why don't you talk to the Anima or the Shadow?" Use your dynamic imagination and visualization during meditation. Take a piece of paper and a pencil, and after you have done your relaxation meditation and you find yourself more centered, speak to the Anima as if it were a person. Ask, "What are you trying to tell me?" Write down the very first things that come to your mind. You can do this with the Shadow also. If you are not afraid of the Shadow, then you can work with it. Remember that the information you receive is metaphorical and not to be interpreted literally or superstitiously. Decoding and interpreting such metaphors can be made clearer with the help of an experienced guide.

Exercise 10: Dream Meditation

Dreams are a way, like free association, for information from the True Self to be communicated to the Ego Self without interference from the Ego's defenses. Say to yourself, "I want to understand myself better and I know that my dreams often communicate to me the things that I need to know." Take a notebook or a piece of paper and pencil. Put them beside your nightstand. When you wake from a dream, write it down immediately; if you don't, you tend to forget most of it. If you have a hard time remembering your dream, it is often not worth remembering and you need not concern yourself with it. If, however, when you wake up you can recall the dream, or at least a great part of it, there is something there that could be useful.

Write it all out. Then you can go through the dream very carefully. This is very important. Ask every part of the dream, "What are you trying to tell me?" Say there is a blue sky and a brown building in the dream. Ask the blue sky, "What are you trying to tell me? What does the blue sky represent?" You ask the brown building, "What do you represent, what are you trying to tell me?" Ask any individuals in the story what they represent.

Last of all, ask yourself, "What part of this dream did I most associate with, and to what part of the dream do I most have an aversion?" These parts of the dream can help you have a great deal of insight into what is happening in your psyche. Again the idea is that the psyche is constantly seeking homeostasis and harmony. We say that the True Self is seeking and calling out to the Ego Self. We are being lured into wholeness. Through the imagination, through the libido, through creativity, through the dark energy, our True Self is always trying to bring us to wholeness. There is nothing within us that is going to be cut off. Everything stays. It is just a matter of orientation and understanding. There are a lot of other techniques, but these are the basic ones that I utilize.

Personality Types

Here is another tool that we can use to help us in our interactions with others. All people have personality traits which, when discerned and understood, can help us relate to one another. Psychologists have many different models they have created in order to try and create a map of the personality.

For our purposes, we simply point out that some folks are more introverted and others are extroverted. Some are more intellectual and others are more emotional. The introvert has a rich inner life and in social settings prefers the company of a few, finding large gatherings draining, while the extrovert prefers the outer life and socializing, finding that this public interaction is stimulating. Those who are more intellectual may tend to pay less attention to their emotional life and need to become more mindful of its importance, while those who are more emotionally inclined may require the balance of rational discourse. In either case, it is important to see our personality orientations not as fixed, but as results of conditioning that can be understood and seen more clearly, helping us to grow more balanced. Understanding these differences can also allow us see how others learn and respond differently, allowing us to adjust and clarify our expectations.

Additionally, we can also understand each other better by recognizing that each individual falls into a vocational orientation that can be defined as either "The Hunter" or "The Farmer". The Hunter is someone who prefers novelty and constant change in his or her vocation and is a "big picture" person; whereas, the Farmer prefers regularity, routine and details. Having a basic understanding of our personality traits can not only help us to better discern our own sense of direction, but can aid us in better communication.

Chapter Four
The Third Direction: Harnessing the Power of the True Self

The Third Direction is where we really begin to focus on mindfulness or clear-seeing practice. The first two directions are more meditation oriented, but the Third Direction is where we begin to get into analytical and insight practice. There are no new models to learn and we can begin to take our practice into our everyday experience.

Exercise 11: The Four Steps of Mindfulness

The most basic technique in the Third Direction is the Four Steps of Mindfulness practice. You can use this technique any time you experience a bothersome emotion or feeling that becomes very strong. It gives you a way to deal with it at the moment that it arises. You can free yourself from the chain of reactions to the thought. You do not have to sabotage yourself and start a whole cascade of offensive negative thinking, feeling, action, and of course, consequences. Again, all of our practices are about freedom.

Four Steps of Mindfulness
1.) Say to yourself, "This negative feeling or thought is coming from my Ego Self, not my True Self."
2.) Say, "I can be clear and free of these thoughts and feelings."
3.) Focus on a meditative practice, the 4Questions (see below) or practice conscious, temporary suppression.
4.) Take time to reaffirm and take refuge in the practices of mindfulness.

Hey Joe!
Joe is walking along and all of a sudden something jogs a negative memory and he remembers being bullied as a child. Joe begins to feel very upset and perhaps gets very angry or full of fear.

The First Step of Mindfulness is for him to recognize that these thoughts and feelings are coming from his conditioned self rather than his clear, true nature of mind. He makes a very clear distinction that this is not coming from his True Self but rather his conditioned self. This is very important because Joe now begins to mindfully disassociate from things that damage. This process is a continuation of what we talked about earlier where you learn not to say, "I am depressed," but rather, "I'm having depressive feelings but I am not depressed." We begin to dissociate or make a separation between being and having, between being and doing. So Joe says to himself, "I am okay, I'm just having a painful memory and my hurt child is expressing itself."

The Second Step of Mindfulness is to affirm that you can be clear and free of the conditioning that doesn't benefit you. You can affirm that with this type of practice, the "you" that can see clearly where thoughts are coming from inevitably frees you from the negative feelings. So Joe says, "I am no longer a powerless child, I am an empowered adult!"

The Third Step of Mindfulness involves actually taking action. There are several ways you can do this. One way is to practice conscious suppression. At this stage you can say to yourself, "I know that this is not coming from my True Self. It's coming from my negative conditioning. I can be free and clear right now. I don't have the time for meditation or practice right now but I can do that later in the day. I can take this material into my meditation period and figure it out then."

Suppression is a temporary, conscious act. We are temporarily putting something off to deal with it at a more appropriate time. If, on the other hand, we try to ignore it and never deal with it then that would become repression, which is an unconscious and unfortunately, sometimes life-long reaction. This is a negative thing because the psyche is a closed universe; those energies have to be dealt with at some point. If they are not dealt with, they can become part of the Shadowy material of our psyche.

Another technique in the Third Step of Mindfulness is to just simply practice walking meditation or sitting meditation by focusing on the breath or mantra. You do not want to push away thoughts or feelings or your own aversions to them. You also do the practice that we started in the Second Direction, which included observer meditation and enlightened self-talk. The steps build on each other and ought to be done in this pattern. If you jump from one to the other you are probably not going to have sufficient time to develop efficiency or effectiveness in using the practices. That is why they are called practices! We need to practice them.

The Fourth Step of Mindfulness comes when you realize that that thought or feeling has passed, even a little. It will pass because that is the stabilizing, understanding nature of mind. No thought or feeling remains constant. There is a continual rising and falling of feelings, thoughts and sensations. Once it has passed a little bit, we affirm again that this practice is working and then take refuge in it once more. This is another form of affirmation like step two, only this time we are affirming that the practice works. This is so important because it is the psyche's job to make little demarcations from our experiences, to say that this is a different or new way to be. In other words *the psyche begins to unconsciously change along with the conscious direction that we give.* We can also begin to create a subconscious subroutine. Our new sub-programming begins to tell us, "You know that this works," and begins to change the way that the psyche functions into a much more clear, clean and whole process.

These are the Four Steps of Mindfulness. Joe experiences a lightness and freedom from his troubling thoughts. He realizes that he no longer has to be a victim of the past and that any problem that arises is in the present and can be dealt with by utilizing compassion borne of the wisdom arising from clarity.

Exercise 12: The Four Questions of Mindfulness

The next technique used in the Third Direction is called the *Four Questions of Mindfulness*. This is probably the heart of the practice in terms of mindfulness. First, I again recommend that you keep a journal of your reflections. Writing or talking about your thoughts really changes the way that the brain processes the thoughts. It is similar to creating a subroutine. It also allows you to go back over time and see how you have been progressing. When you look back at journal entries over a year when you were in the deep throes of depression or anxiety, you may be really shocked that you believed those unclear thoughts and felt and behaved out of them. It is another step of affirmation in developing a whole new way of thinking and feeling.

The Four Questions process itself is relatively simple but it does take some practice. The first part of the method is to take a troubling situation that arises in your life and use the experience to complete the pictured chart.

Situation: Write down a paragraph about a situation that keeps coming into your thoughts						
Sensation: At least 1 body sensation (sick, skin hot, stomach or shoulders tight etc.) [Rate 1-10]						
Emotion: At least 4 emotions, these will be rated from scale of 1-10 (10 highest)						
Emotion	Rating	Emotion	Rating	Emotion	Rating	
Thought (Rate 1-10) List the thoughts that created the strongest emotion and rated from scale of 1-10 (10 highest)	Rating	**Question 1:** What is not clear about the thought (real, rational, rewarding, not completely true)?	**Question 2:** What belief or basic programming model created this thought?	**Question 3:** Do you think anyone else has ever had this experience?	**Question 4:** What would it mean if this thought were actually true and what creative action could you take?	

Compile your answers to the Four Questions and create a new and clear thought to challenge the old one.
When the exercise is completed take an inventory of how your feelings have changed about the situation. [Write in the space below]

For example, Joe is checking out in a supermarket and he sees a person in front of him that he used to be very close to, and it triggers troubling memories. At that point he can practice the Four Steps of Mindfulness because he doesn't have time to do anything further about it. Later in the day when Joe sits in his evening meditation, he takes out his journal and writes out the incident following the steps of the Four Questions of Mindfulness.

Situation: Write down a paragraph about a situation that keeps coming into your thoughts
I saw Katie at the supermarket this afternoon and my mind was flooded with painful memories of the day that we broke up

Sensation: At least 1 body sensation (sick, skin hot, stomach or shoulders tight etc.) [Rate 1-10]
Flushed (5)

Emotion: At least 4 emotions, these will be rated from scale of 1-10 (10 highest)

Emotion	Rating	Emotion	Rating	Emotion	Rating
Anger	10	Frustration	5		
Sadness	7	Confusion	6		

Thought (Rate 1-10) List the thoughts that created the strongest emotion and rated from scale of 1-10 (10 highest)	Rating	Question 1: What is not clear about the thought (real, rational, rewarding, not completely true)?	Question 2: What belief or basic programming model created this thought?	Question 3: Do you think anyone else has ever had this experience?	Question 4: What would it mean if this thought were actually true and what creative action could you take?
I feel like a loser	8	The fact that the relationship with Katie didn't work out doesn't mean that I am a loser. I can improve my relationship skills. This doesn't say anything about my worth as a human being. Also, it takes two to make a relationship work or fail	Critical Parent Hurt inner child conditioning	Yes. Everyone feels this way sometimes, even Katie	My self-esteem comes from my being not doing and having. I can work on my relationship skills without having to be perfect.
Katie is lie a symbol of everthing that is wrong with my life	7				
I'm terrible at relationships. I deserve to be alone	10				

Compile your answers to the Four Questions and create a new and clear thought to challenge the old one.
When the exercise is completed take an inventory of how your feelings have changed about the situation. [Write in the space below]

My worth doesn't depend on the success of a relationship. We have all had troubled relationships. No one is so lely responsible for the success or failure of any relationship. I can work on relationship skills without having to be perfect

    He begins by describing the situation as simply and distinctly as he can. I ask people to be specific about when it happened because sometimes you can see patterns. There may be certain times in the day or certain types of associations that tend to trigger negative thoughts and feelings. You then realize that you can begin to avoid those or begin to more creatively work around them. For example, Joe notices that many of his troubling moods occur in the evening. This tells him that he does not want to do anything stressful in the evening that he really wants to rework his schedule so that he is able to relax during the evening and not focus or dwell on problems. He needs to shift problem-solving activities to the morning or afternoon.

    Next, Joe asks himself, "What were the feelings you noticed?" He uses mindfulness to help orient or bring him back, to help him be aware of what was going on. He writes down his feelings and physical sensations, such as flushed, uncomfortable, angry, sad or confused. Writing those feelings and emotions down brings the left hemisphere of the brain into play. When Joe has named all of the feelings that he experienced, he takes a deep breath. Because mind states and the breath are interconnected, sometimes after a deep breath a hidden feeling will surface.

    Now Joe numbers the feelings from 1 to 10 in terms of their intensity. Once again it is important for him to do free association with the numbers. Joe picks the first number that pops into his head. This allows him to get more efficiently to the root of what is bothering him without his ego defenses distracting him. If, when Joe looks back over his numbers, he finds that the two strongest feelings are both a 10, he just asks himself which is stronger. That feeling stays a 10; the other becomes a 9.

When he finds out which one is the highest, he can begin to work with it. One of the unique things that you find about mindfulness is that it has a domino effect. If you work with the root feeling, the other ones usually clear up by themselves. If anything is under a 5, it is usually not strong enough to worry about.

Once Joe discovers which feeling is the strongest, let us say for example anger, he writes down the thoughts that are driving the anger. Remember, we know that it is impossible for the feeling to occur without having a thought first. The source of the feeling was the thought that created it. Again, Joe takes a deep breath to free up any hidden thoughts. Number each of the thoughts from 1 to 10 to find out which thought was the strongest. Now we can get down to the root cause.

First Question of Mindfulness

Next Joe challenges his strongest thought (I'm terrible at relationships and deserve to be alone.) with mindfulness. He asks himself, "Is there anything about the thought that is not true?" What distortions or delusions might there be in that thought? For one thing, his relationship issues are about *doing* and *having,* not a statement about his *being*. His ability to be in a good relationship is an ego skill, which he can work to improve, but he cannot improve or detract from his True Nature. That is the first distortion or delusion. He can write that in First Question column.

Furthermore, he can ask what is not realistic or rational about the thought. Joe realizes that he actually has many good relationships in his life with family and friends; therefore, it is neither a statement about reality nor rational to say the he is terrible at relationships.

He can also ask if the thought is helpful. In some situations it may be difficult to ascertain what is not true about a thought and determining whether or not it is helpful may be more powerful. Joe realizes that his thought is not helpful because it makes him feel badly about himself and doesn't motivate him to improve.

Lastly, he can take an existential position and ask, "What would this say about me if it were true?" This questioning can often lead to a hidden thought that is perceived as an attack on our very being. For example, Joe might uncover this hidden thought: my very being is worthless and I deserve to be alone. This hidden thought is the underlying reason that the situation bothered him so much; it was an attack not on his doing or having, but on his very being.

One of the things we find in mindfulness practice which surprises many people is that *99 percent of the time the troubling situation in which we find ourselves is not really about us personally*. And even when the other person involved says it is about us, they are usually projecting some aspect of their own psyche. In fact, many of the situations you assumed were about you probably in reality had little to do with you. For example, Joe is not even sure that his difficulties with his past lovers were really just about him. The reality of the situation is that it takes both persons to make a relationship work or fail. He can now put these clarifying thoughts in the First Question column.

Second Question of Mindfulness

In the Second Question Joe will review the mindfulness models in order to understand how he has been conditioned and to reaffirm the clearer, more mindful attitude that he has freely and consciously adopted. For example, Joe might ask himself if perfectionism was involved in his reaction to this situation. He realizes that while he has many good relationships, he was very disturbed about this one that didn't work out because it offended his belief that he had achieved some sort of perfection. He reminds himself that perfection is an unachievable goal that he is no longer striving for; wholeness is a better option.

In addition, he realizes that his thought that he is terrible at relationships is coming from his critical parent conditioning and the thought that he deserves to be alone is coming from his hurt inner child. Together they form his adaptive conditioning which causes him to blame himself for everything, creating a shield that, while meant to protect him and allow him to avoid really dealing with the problem, in reality doesn't allow him to grow. He was conditioned to think this way when he was very young. He is now going to decide for himself how to interpret his experiences.

Third Question of Mindfulness

In the Third Question Joe will want to take the ego out of the situation a little bit and ask himself, always starting with the pronoun *we,* "Is there something about my strongest thought (I'm terrible at relationships and I deserve to be alone.) that we all can relate to? In other words, if Joe asked a dozen people randomly on the street if they ever had the experience of feeling as if they were terrible at relationships and deserved to be alone, is it possible that the majority of those people might say yes? Of course it is. This question is like a mirror that reflects the thought and takes us out of the egocentric realm, reminding us that our experiences are universal. In a fascinating way, it also helps us to feel more connected.

Fourth Question of Mindfulness

The next part of this exercise is the most difficult, but it also can be the most freeing. This question helps us to develop a deep sense of mature self-acceptance. By asking, "What would it mean if my thought were true? What would it say about me? How has this situation affected my sense of self-esteem?" Joe could come to the understanding that every emotional hook that digs deeply does so because we falsely believe it is an attack on our sense of self worth and our very being. To counter this, Joe can utilize the True Self Esteem Mindfulness Model and affirm his new orientation. He reminds himself that we all feel terrible at relationships sometimes and that's okay. Sometimes things just don't work out; this is a universal experience that everyone can relate to. Additionally, in this particular case, Joe did not even know for sure why his relationship didn't succeed. He does, however, know that he has a history of blaming himself for things without having all the facts, and that this could be a component of this situation.

The last part of the Four Questions is to come up with some experimental action that Joe can take to effect a full realization and shift in consciousness. Our formula for this is:

Insight + Experimental Creative Action = Realization

The most important quality of the creative action is the experimental aspect. This shifts us away from looking for a perfect answer and allows us to come up with a heuristic or working model. Because it is an experiment, it may need to be changed slightly or even completely depending upon the situation. By seeing more clearly, and understanding more deeply, the appropriate healing actions will naturally arise. In the example above, Joe could begin to practice Reorientation Meditation to affirm a new view of his self worth and spend time going over the various mindfulness models of the Four Directions System. Finally, he could speak with persons who care about him and who know him well, asking for honest feedback about his relationship issues.

Once you have completed the 4Q chart, you can put the insights together to form *a new, harmonious thought*. In our example, we know what Joe went through, and we realize that everybody has had the experience of feeling like a failure, but the truth is that our success or failure is not something that we accomplish alone. It is always a joint venture. In addition, Joe realizes that he has many positive relationships in his life and so maintaining these is not an either/or proposition. Sometimes relationships work and sometimes they don't. It is not realistic to think that all of our relationships will work out. Finally, maintaining a relationship is a skill that can be improved if we, through clarity, find it to be necessary.

Now he has put those insights together and has a new clear thought to challenge the old one. He can then ask himself, when he looks at the harmony column, how much does he believe that this thought is a reflection of the way things really are. Note that we ask not the way he wishes they were or the way he wishes they were not, but just a mirror to reality. Then we use the 1 to 10 again, 10 being total reality. What Joe is going to find is that the harmony thought is the closest to actual reality. If it is not a 10, it's at least a 9. When he looks back at his old thought and asks himself how much that old thought represents reality, it becomes very easy to see that it is very low, probably close to a 2, and that it reflects more his feelings than it does reality.

The Four Questions of Mindfulness is a very precise technique and it is important to work your way through all of the questions in order. After the practice, Joe can ask himself if he feels worse having done the exercise, the same, or a little bit better. Even if he feels just a tiny bit better, it is important that he recognizes that. Clarifying his thoughts will always clarify his feelings. Joe might have to repeat this practice if he feels only slightly better. Usually by the second or third time he will notice a shift and feel considerably better.

Again, it is important to take the time to go through the entire process and not skip any questions; if you do, you do not really get the full benefit. The more time you devote to going through the practice, the more you realize, "Wow, this really works!"

and you continue to do it for each new instance that arises. As you practice, you will become more proficient and able to complete the process more quickly, but be patient, cognitive restructuring takes time! In fact, you will probably discover that the 4Q process is one of the most dynamic practices in your mindfulness toolkit.

Chapter Five
The Fourth Direction: Trusting in the True Self

The last Direction is closely related to the first. It is probably the easiest and in some ways the most difficult. This last step is about cultivating faith or trust in the idea of the True Self. Through practicing the first three Directions, you will realize that there is a great advantage to the practice of mindfulness and understanding the dynamic of the *True Self/Ego Self* relationship. By learning to distinguish between the self-confidence issues of the ego and the inherent nature of our self-worth, we can begin to more freely explore our ego issues and make the changes that bring about a joyful experience of being.

Whether the True Self exists only as a metaphor or not, orienting yourself this way and adopting the philosophy of finding your self-worth inherently rather than basing it on doing and having is incredibly practical and frees you up. You are feeling better, but taking the next step by starting to rely on the True Self is what the Fourth Direction is all about.

There are two ways to go about the practice of cultivating this awakened heart or trust. I put these two practices together into a very simple form. Essentially you begin to see the True Self not just as a pragmatic philosophy or experiment or as a way to approach things psychologically, but as something real, something that has always been there in an infinite, ancient way and is always available to you. This allows the Ego Self to relax into its embrace. Sometimes it is as simple as saying, "I don't know what to do, please help me, True Self."

The first practice in cultivating trust in the True Self is the positive affirmation practice; it is very powerful. Using the imagination, allow your Ego Self to have a conversational relationship with the True Self. Allow the Ego Self to express its fears and its desires openly to the True Self and allow that part of you, that child part of you, to completely let go and express itself.

One of the affirmations that we use at The Center for Mindful Living is: "Breath by Breath, trusting in the True Self, every world is my world." This verse helps us to realize that when we experience great change and the new "world" that we find ourselves in seems alien or foreign, we need to affirm that we are always connected and that we always belong, all of us alone, together.

What you will find in the True Self, and this is indeed how you will know it is the True Self, is that there is always compassion expressed first. The True Self responds spontaneously with compassion. Remember the model about the parent, adult and child? Compassion is coming from the adult via the True Self. When we are communicating with the True Self, saying, "Oh, I'm just so afraid this is going to happen" or, "Man, I really want this to happen," when we sit down and have that inner dialogue, the first thing that comes through us is compassion. When we feel that compassion coming through us, we know we are in touch with our True Self, our True Nature.

When your dialogue is immediately critical or in problem-solving mode, then it is not coming from your True Self. The first thing we should receive is compassion. This also shows us that this is the best way to communicate with other people, to be compassionate with them first. Without that, they are not going to be open to anything that we have to offer in terms of reason or wisdom.

The second way that we can practice living from the True Self is to really just begin to trust it to take care of things. There is a hurt, fearful part of us, that says, "I can't take this anymore!" and wants to give up. There is another part of us that wants to say, "I'm not going to take this anymore!" and wants to fight back. But there is a third part of us that says, "I can take anything that you throw at me." This is our True Self, our inner creative intelligence, the part of us that can handle anything, knows how to deal with anything in both the most terrible and the best situations. We have to cultivate and learn to trust it.

We do this in little ways. Usually the first experience a person has with this is working with me through an issue or problem. First they just take this trusting on as an idea. Eventually they begin to see that it is something they can rely on. Part of it is practicing what is called the wisdom of "Not Knowing" and not seeing the unknown as something negative. The reality in which we all live is that there are a great many things that we really don't know. By consciously entering into that Not Knowing with trust in our True Self, we can have the courage to be patient and to continue to persevere. We begin to see that there are only solutions and that those solutions are only going to come from our True Self. This is a process I call *lucid clarification.*

For example, let us say Jodie finds herself in a difficult marriage. To deal with this she may quickly try moving on to another relationship, only to find that she is facing the same issues with a different partner (wherever you go, there you are). Instead, Jodie could practice not knowing and take a 'time-out' to exert some creative energy working on her own personal issues and then, only after she feels she has gained some real insight, make a decision about her current relationship.

It may take time to find the solution, but cultivating the fourth practice, which is to nurture reliance in the True Self, is probably the most powerful thing that we can do, and once we do it, *all of the other practices seem easier.*

Exercise 13: "Just Being" Meditation

Once you really understand trusting in the True Self purely and clearly, all of the other practices of mindfulness become like magic, and they become much easier to do. Your practice of meditation and mindfulness moves from being a technical problem-solving activity to something that is very beautiful and enriches your life. Sitting meditation becomes a pronouncement that your Being is the ground of your worth. You can just sit there. You do not have to do anything; just be. You can embrace the mystery of being. You just plant your metaphorical flag in the ground saying, "My being is enough, and I don't have to do anything to prove my worth." Mindfulness becomes a way to open up to previously unknown depths of joy, understanding, and happiness and realize that we are all interconnected in ways that we can never fully appreciate when we are just focusing on our own problems.

Together the Four Directions move in a circle going into the center and back out in an ongoing process. This is the way that we move through our lives. Eventually as we go through those five stages we find we can integrate and find harmony with each of them, although it might take some time. In The Four Directions there is the sense that we have time, we practice and re-awaken. If we do not get it now, we will get it later, but also there is an urgency to do the practices now, as in the admonition, "Time is fleeting; do not hold back. Appreciate this precious life."

Our initial problem that we come to the practice with does not usually take very long for us to resolve in some way. However, working through the five aggregates described in Chapter One can take a while. The practice becomes not about something that is only useful for solving problems, but also about the joy of understanding and the happiness that comes from clarity.

Chapter Six
The Living Mandala: Stories Along the Way

The ancient sage known historically as the Buddha once said, "Do not trust in a teaching only because it is from a sacred book, or only because it comes from an esteemed lineage; test all teachings for yourself as a goldsmith purifies his metal by fire." I completely agree with this wisdom, and that is why I would like to share a few true stories with you that dramatically illustrate what is possible with these mindfulness practices. Over the past three millennia they have been tried, tested and found true. Read for yourself how each direction forms a living mandala or sacred circle of wisdom and compassion.

The First Direction: Ray

This first story helps illustrate the First Direction practice of Reorientation. The idea of Reorientation is moving away from the Ego Self as our center to the True Self as our center, allowing the Ego Self to relax into the embrace of the True Self.

The story that I like to use to illustrate Reorientation is the story of Ray. Ray is a fellow I got to know when I was running a halfway house in a small city in western Pennsylvania.

I had put together an idea for a halfway house after working with both state and federal prisons for many years and doing meditation programs. While talking to one of the prison psychologists whom I had befriended, I asked if there was anything further I could do to help these guys in prison besides doing meditation and some mindfulness counseling.

She replied that there were a lot of nonviolent offenders that could get out of prison on good behavior (for being a good prisoner, so to speak) if they had a family member or somebody on the outside willing to take an interest in them, giving them a place to stay until they could get back on their feet. However, many of them did not have family or anybody that wanted anything to do with them. They would do their maximum time unless someone could vouch for them in the outside world. She said that if I could create a halfway house, it would help some of these men to have a surrogate community, which could aid them in making their way back into society.

I went right to work and I was able to get a couple of business people interested. My father and his partner put the money together, and we bought a house. We worked with the state prison system and became an independent halfway house with ten apartments. The men would stay there and go through a process in which they were required to see me several days a week for counseling. They were also expected to fulfill requirements such as getting a job, continuing their education or attending drug and alcohol counseling.

One of the first arrivals was a fellow by the name of Ray. Ray was in his sixties, and he had spent most of his life in prison. He was finishing a stint of almost 20 years when he came to my attention. I myself was only in my late twenties. Ray was a really interesting guy. He reminded me of an aging Clint Eastwood kind of character, very cool, very quiet with a raspy voice. He had been a professional thief all his life, but he never behaved violently and never carried a gun or any kind of weapon. His son was in prison at the time as well for similar crimes.

He came to the house right off the bus from the prison. Ray was a very tough guy, and he had a hard side to him, as you can imagine of anyone who spent so much time in prison. When Ray arrived at our house I interviewed him and gave him a room. The very next day one of the guys that had been there a while came over to my office and said that Ray had threatened his life. Ray had taken a big bowie knife that he had purchased at a sporting goods store and stuck it in the doorjamb of his neighbor's door, informing him that if he didn't turn his radio off or stop playing it so loudly, he was going to come in and cut his throat.

That was my first experience with Ray, so of course I had to talk to him about it immediately. I left a note on his door for him to see me that day in my office. He came over, and I explained to him that that kind of behavior would not be accepted. He started to give me some grief about it. I was just very straight with him and said, "Look, I will not tolerate violence or threats of any kind in this house and if you don't like it, go back to prison, because I'm not having it here." It was fairly awkward because he was so much older than I was. I think he was impressed by the fact that I was not afraid of him or put off by his demeanor.

He never gave me any trouble after that, except once when a couple of younger guys came through that were Hispanic and black. There was a real difference in terms of their ages compared to Ray. Younger guys were a bit more aggressive and less respectful than the older residents.

Ray came over and said, "I'm not going to share any space with a black punk. I didn't want to in prison and I'm not doing it here."

I said, "Well, let me ask you something; how would you like me to treat you? Do you want me to treat you based on who people think you are because of your background, or would you rather that I treat you based on my actual experience of you?" Of course he didn't say anything. I said, "Well then, I want you to extend the same to these fellows. You don't know them. I want you to just try to base all of your thoughts of them only on your experience of them and try to let go of who you think they are because of where they come from or the color of their skin." I said again that I would not tolerate that kind of behavior at this house; everybody gets an equal start. I could tell that Ray wasn't happy with this but he nodded in agreement and silently slid out of my office.

Ray had no psychological background, but he knew that I was a mindfulness teacher. He began to be curious and to ask me about the practices, so we started to practice not just the counseling aspect but also meditation. One of the main practices that I talked about was this idea of Reorientation, which Ray started to do. It became his main custom, setting up his little altar space and having an object at the center as his True Self, and starting to bow to that part of himself. Ray started to reorient and recognize that his center was coming from his True Self and not from his Ego Self.

Ray really took to it. I don't know if it was because of his age or the need, or having nothing to lose, but here was this guy in his sixties who had never had any kind of exposure to this way of thinking before, working with this young twenty-something, and we really connected. He really took to these teachings, and I saw a transformation take place that was really miraculous. He went from being this hard-nosed, squinty-eyed don't trust anybody, everybody's a son of a bitch guy, to this man who actually became a model for the rest of the residents in the house.

I began to notice things about Ray that he had learned in prison. When you're in prison, you live in a very small room, and so space becomes very important to you. For Ray that meant that when you came to his door, you took off your shoes. His room was immaculate and very neat, and he also wore very basic simple clothes. He wore dungarees and a white T-shirt with a blue jean jacket, very simple.

I would come to his room in the morning on occasion and we would go to breakfast together, and he would take his time getting ready. Sometimes I would find him shaving, and even the way he took care of his toiletries was done with great attention. He used an old-fashioned shaving brush. I can still remember the scent.

There was something always clean and clear about Ray, and when he combined it with his practice of Reorientation Meditation it seemed like all these little things came together. For example, when he went with me to the Burger King, he would always get a cheeseburger and a cup of black coffee, and he would unfold the wrapper and put everything neatly in its place. He would very mindfully take time to eat, and when he was eating, he wouldn't talk to you. He would listen, but he wouldn't speak when he was eating. When he had finished a bite and taken a drink, then maybe he would say something. It reminded me of the mindfulness admonition, "When you eat, just eat."

All these little things about him that he learned living in prison, all these little things that for some people may not be very significant, became manifestations of his True Self. It was as if I were witnessing an old Zen monk come to life.

Eventually I began to give Ray more responsibility because I saw that he was a natural leader, and I needed that to keep order at the house. I made him the caretaker. He would report to me on different problems, things that needed to be taken care of, like basic carpentry. As time passed we became very close to each other. He had a real zest for life as evidenced by the fact that at 67 years of age he met and dated a younger woman who could not have been much older than I was.

He was a very vigorous guy, and I grew to love him very much. Unfortunately, I didn't know that he had heart condition, or maybe it was just coming on, but one day he didn't show up for our morning meeting. I went over to the house, which was only a block or two away from my office. I knocked on the door. Usually I'd smell the aftershave or the soap from his shower, but there was none of that. Because I had keys to all the rooms, I opened up the door. He was lying there on the bed face down, having died of a heart attack. I remember being very saddened by that event, but at the same time I remember seeing the body there and remembering that that body was not Ray. His spirit was much bigger than his temporary self, and he'd simply outgrown that old form.

He had given directions to one of his friends that he wanted to be cremated and have me perform his funeral. It was beautiful. Some friends of his attended: homeless people and street people that he had been watching out for, and people who lived downtown. About 10 or 12 of us gathered, and we talked about Ray. I gave everybody the opportunity to share what Ray meant to him or her, and I shared with everyone what he meant to me.

One of the older women that Ray had befriended approached me after the service was over and we had scattered his ashes at the river. She said that Ray had really grown to love me and feel proud of me, and he felt as if I were the son that he had never really had. He and Israel, his biological son, had always been distant from each other both geographically and emotionally. They had never really known each other. I remember I wrote a letter to Ray's son in prison and his daughter-in-law and granddaughter informing them that he had passed away but also making sure that they knew what kind of man he had become.

    I always think of old Ray and how much he taught me, but especially how much he showed me that it doesn't matter how old you are, where you come from, or what you experience. *Everyone can change, because none of those identities is fixed.* Ray became the person that he always was deep down inside, and his True Self really came through.

The Second Direction: Mary
    The second story illustrates the sitting practice and how sitting meditation and learning to observe our thoughts and feelings and sensations are another part of practicing freedom. This is the story of a woman who was referred to me by a doctor friend.

    Mary suffered from postpartum depression after giving birth to her second child. It was a very difficult time for her. Not only had she developed depression, but prior to that she also developed a very severe case of obsessive-compulsive disorder (OCD). She had, for the most part, an obsessive thought disorder rather than the compulsive behaviors that people sometimes display like washing their hands or checking things repeatedly. Her obsessions took the form of horrible images that would appear in her mind when she got near her baby. She thought that if she touched the baby, somehow she would hurt it or it would catch on fire.

    Mary knew that this was irrational and that she would never harm her baby, but these thoughts kept going through her mind over and over again, and she seemed to have no control over them. It was getting to the point where it was paralyzing her and she was no longer able to care for the child. She had to have her sister care for the baby, and then she became very depressed because she couldn't get control of the problem. The doctor wanted to put her on medication to help with the obsessive thoughts but she adamantly refused.

    Mary came to me very depressed, suffering greatly from this problem. I explained to her the development of the five stages and how sometimes pregnancy will trigger major hormonal and chemical changes in the body that can cause these disorders; obviously that was the case in her situation. I explained that usually there is some endogenous predisposition to having OCD. Sometimes initially it is not a big problem; however, an experience such as giving birth can cause chemical changes that will make the condition more severe.

    Concerning these terrible images, I explained that at the heart of them, whether a person has to count to six every time he or she goes past a certain door, or whether one has to touch something a number of times when going past it, or as in her case that if she touches someone that she will hurt the person in some fashion, they are all coming from the same negative conditioning. In Mary's case, what was behind these terrible images was that deep down, she had a poor view of herself and was very confused about her self-esteem. This situation had been created in her earlier life when she was the black sheep of the family and consequently formed a negative view of herself. Her obsessive images metaphorically reflected this. I also explained to her that because she was so paralyzed with fear and panic, she would never in reality follow through with these actions; they were just obsessive thoughts, not things that she would consciously choose to act on. I explained to her the power of volition and that she would not act contrary to her will.

This helped her. Understanding a situation always helps people significantly. Yet she was still being barraged by these thoughts day in and day out. I began to put her through the stages of practice. When we got to the Second Direction and started sitting meditation with focusing on the breath or on a mantra, she really seemed to turn the corner. By realizing that she could observe her thoughts, she could just let them be there. Normally she would push them away, which only made them worse, or go into them and say, "Why am I having these thoughts? There must be something terribly wrong with me."

I said to her, "That's an attachment or aversion. Aversion is trying to push the thoughts away, and that doesn't work. Attachment is going into the thoughts and just getting more deluded and more distorted as a result." I instructed her to avoid pushing the thoughts away, just to experience them, label them as thoughts and then go back to the breath or mantra.

She started doing this and would sit for 20 minutes two times a day. She discovered that during her sitting period she actually found that there was a little bit of space where she could just let that terrible thought arise in her head and not push it away or go into it. She could label it as a thought and associate just with her awareness and not with the troubling image.

Mary began to experience a space free from her thoughts. At first, that space was very small but it became bigger and bigger. She found that when an obsessive thought came up she was able to do the Four Steps of Mindfulness. She would simply say to herself, "This is just a negative thought coming from my conditioned self, not my True Self; I can be free and clear of this." Then she would do her meditation, usually a traditional one where she would walk or sit. When the space got big enough and the thought was no longer there, then she would reaffirm to herself that this practice was working. Mary got to the place where she began to have almost a sense of amusement because she knew that even the most fantastic images had no real power over her.

In about three months she went from having recorded, by her own account, 15 to 20 episodes of obsessive thoughts every day to only once or twice a day. At that point we began to go deeper into her personal situation and uncover the roots of her terrible self-esteem. Through the practices we were able to completely rid her of the hurtful thoughts. She was free!

I did explain to her that at some point obsessive thoughts might return and might have a different complexion. She did not need to see this as something negative, but as something positive. The OCD is telling you that there is something going on deep within your thoughts that is unclear or distorted. The obsessions themselves can be turned inside out and seen as a mindfulness bell.

OCD is a terrible disorder; I was also able to convince her to consider using a serotonin medication that would help with the chemical imbalance that she was experiencing. She ultimately enjoyed complete freedom from the obsessions. It was a very powerful experience for her. I always share this story as a way to explain how *the practice of sitting and the practice of labeling our thoughts can be life changing.*

When people downplay OCD I explain to them that it can become almost paralyzing; however, there is a way out of it, a way to freedom, and the way to freedom is in these mindfulness practices.

The Third Direction: Jimmy

The third story illustrates the power of mindfulness as used analytically in the Third Direction. You look at the situation that creates negative feelings, examine the thoughts creating the feelings, and then question or challenge those thoughts with mindfulness. By doing this we can see if thoughts are distorted and try to develop a more clear thought process.

The story I always like to share here concerns a fellow that I worked with in a federal prison some years ago. I was running the meditation and counseling group there. This was a group of guys imprisoned for various reasons, from stealing, to drug dealing, to assault. This one fellow in particular, Jim, had committed rape twice and had mugged and assaulted several people.

I was teaching the practices, and we got to the point of talking about mindfulness and beginning to learn to examine our thoughts. I explained the Third Question and how we try to take ourselves out of a thought and ask if anybody else has had a similar experience. We try to be less egocentric and see through the eyes of other people and thus understand our interrelatedness and interconnectedness.

At this point, Jim, who was normally very quiet, suddenly spoke out and said, "You know, Dr. Stultz, I have to tell you that I have never personally experienced remorse for what I have done."

I asked, "Could you explain more about what you mean?"

He said, "As I'm sitting here listening to people talk about what they did and how they feel bad about it, I have to tell you I do not have any bad feelings about what I did. I remember very clearly beating up some guy and robbing him, and then I'd have a milkshake and a sandwich and never think twice about it. In fact some people label me a sociopath because I'm not able to feel bad about the things that I do."

I said, "Okay. Let's just assume that you aren't able to. Let's assume that either because of your birth genetics or some experience in early life that you really can't experience a negative or bad feeling. The good news from the Mindfulness point of view is that you don't need to feel badly in order to act in an ethical way."

I then said, "Let me illustrate this. Jim, will you put your chair in the center of the circle, please?" So he moved his chair, and I said, pointing to the other inmates, "We are going to stand around Jim. Each of you may pick up your chair." Everybody did so.

"On my command, all of us will take turns hitting Jim over the head with our chairs."

He looked at me and said, "That's crazy!"

I asked, "What's the matter?"

He responded, "Are you serious?"

I said again, "We are all going to take turns smacking Jim in the head with chairs as hard as we can."

He exclaimed, "You're crazy!"

I replied, "What's wrong? I don't understand the problem."

Jim said forcefully, "I don't want to be hit in the head with those chairs."

I told the other guys, "Okay, you can return your chairs to the circle and sit back down." Jim, too, did as I asked.

I explained, "You see, Jim, the reason I did this was to illustrate that even though you may not be able to feel with what people may call 'a conscience,' if we all started to hit you with our chairs you knew it would cause you pain. Even if you were not feeling any fear at that moment, just the knowledge and awareness of the pain that you would experience upset you, is that not true?"

He said, "Yeah, of course."

I continued, "Now, here's the point: those people you robbed and raped, you don't have to feel anything to know that it harmed them."

Jim just stared at me. He didn't say a word. He did not have to feel anything to know that he did not want to be beaten up or raped. You could see the light of awareness in his eyes. He said, "I never thought about it that way; I was always just focused on the fact that I didn't have feelings about it that were negative."

I replied, "Jim, I know it's very easy to put labels such as sociopath on people and say that because a person is impulsive and without any feeling, there is something wrong with him. Maybe on some chemical level there is, but here's the point: to practice non-harming you don't have to feel anything. The virtue of the Four Directions practice is that *you don't have to have a strong feeling in order to not harm someone or to help someone.*"

In other words, for me to show compassion doesn't mean that I have to like a person, hang around him or feel good about him. In fact, I could actually dislike him but still I recognize that none of us wants to suffer, so I know that even that person I dislike wants to avoid suffering. I can be compassionate towards him without liking him. That's the beauty of this whole thing.

Jim got it, and after that experience even some of the guards commented that Jim had become like a new person. That's the power of mindfulness. It can manifest itself in many ways: by challenging our thoughts or by allowing us to see things more clearly and understand relationships more honestly. We are not basing what we do, or what we don't do, on our feelings. Rather, we base it on clarity. In this case, the clarity of our interdependence helped Jim to realize that *harming others is not in harmony with the deeper, symbiotic meaning of life.*

The Fourth Direction: Tony and Christine

The fourth story illustrates the Fourth Direction, cultivating faith or trust in the True Self. It is also related to the first three Directions in that they are really about cultivating a mind that is always ready to see past perceptions to practice "Not Knowing" and bearing witness to our True Nature.

Recall the practices of Mindfulness Affirmations and Just Being, which help each of us to live with an awakened heart. We open up to our fears, desires, and anger and are able to express them, embraced by the safe harbor of compassion and wisdom.

The story that I use to illustrate the Fourth Direction is a recent experience of mine. It has to do with grieving the loss of my sister, Christine. Her untimely death has been one of the most difficult things I've had to deal with in my adult life. However, in terms of my practice, I realized several things.

I remember being with my sister in the hospital where she lay in a coma, her head having been severely injured in a car accident. I would sit in the room and meditate. Sometimes I would chant and then say, "If there's any way possible please, please let her recover. Please don't let her die, please let everything be okay." Then I would return to the chanting.

I didn't ask myself why this happened because one of the things you learn from the practice is to move beyond asking why. The real questions become, "How and what?" When you ask why, you are totally ignorant of your connection to the rest of life. The week that my sister died there was a major earthquake in India. I remember seeing on television this man who had just lost his wife, his children and his parents all in one day and thinking that this was a horrible but natural part of life, and nobody needs to ask why.

Also, I remember expressing my feelings of anger, hope and fear and then going back to chanting. Sometimes I'd just sit in silent meditation, and I'd try to match my breath with the respirator. Every time it took a breath I would take a breath. It was a way of feeling close to Christine and harmonizing with her.

Christine's injuries were too significant, and even though the doctors tried valiantly to save her, it was not to be. She died there in the hospital.

There were many times immediately after that event that I had very deep insights. I remember right before she passed away realizing that pain comes in many different sizes and shapes, but the suffering is all the same. I remember sitting in meditation looking at my arm and suddenly realizing that I could take a match and burn my arm, I could hit it with a hammer or I could cut it with a knife and each would make a different type of pain but the suffering that I experienced would ultimately be the same. I also realized that although I was experiencing this terrible loss of my beloved sister, I had suffered just as much over things not nearly as important. The pain was different, but the suffering was the same. At the root of my suffering was my Ego Self.

In the days and weeks and months that followed Christine's death I would try to practice different techniques, but none of them seemed to be working very well. I was not depressed, but I would go into periods of very deep sadness where I would just weep. I wanted my grieving for Christine to be pure; I wanted to be clear. Many times when I would start to cry about missing her, I would practice mindfulness and realize that there were all kinds of thoughts about my own stuff, my own baggage, and that I was using that pain as an excuse to unload and focus on my own problems. I wanted to miss her and grieve for her honestly and authentically.

I remember a time driving in my truck when a wall of sadness came down on top of me as I started to cry. I cried out loud and said, "True Self, please help me, I don't know what to do. I don't know how to deal with this. I know that you will help me." And that was all there was to it; I suddenly realized at that moment that this infinite True Self, the Ground of my Being, was something that I could never be separated from. Indeed, not even death could separate me from it. All of my life, all of my loved ones, all of my experiences were intimately known and connected through that reality, and therefore I could not ultimately ever be separated. The idea of a separate self is a complete delusion. The truth is that I am deeply interconnected with the universe itself, and this experience that I'm having is not an alien one.

A peace came over me, and I realized that no matter what happened in my life, *I could not be separated from that reality and that the True Self had the resources of radical acceptance, love, compassion and wisdom that I needed.* If I would practice just doing what needed to be done with the patience to wait for the wisdom to come forth and the perseverance to keep going, to ride on, then it would be okay. As I went deeper into that experience, all of the practices that weren't working suddenly began to work as if a switch had been turned on.

I still deeply love and miss my sister. I miss her every day, but now when I miss her, I really miss her and it is not tied up with a whole assortment of other issues. When I think about her I don't think so much about the sadness or the separation, as she is still a part of me everyday. I think about what her life meant and about the kind of person she was, how devoted she was to others. Finally, I think about how much of a teacher she was to me and about her caring and kindness.

Chapter Seven
Coming Full Circle

One of the things that a practitioner of mindfulness learns is that all of the practices flow in an interconnected, on-going journey around and within the Four Directions, always leading to and going through the center of our True Self. We can cultivate this relationship to the True Self by the simple practice of *thinking of the True Self as a part of us, a spiritual power within that we can speak to and be with, and who knows us and understands us.* It is very intimate. By developing a very personal sense of that relationship with our transpersonal True Nature, we can tell it all the things that we want; we can tell it all the things we are afraid of. We can trust that no matter what, wisdom and compassion will be there.

Again I remember one of my teachers saying that there are three basic attitudes: I can't take this anymore. I'm not going to take this anymore. Finally, the middle way: I can take anything you throw at me; I can handle anything. The first and second attitudes come from the child in us that has been hurt. A lot of the "not taking this anymore" attitude is a striking out at those above us. The middle way attitude, however, comes from our True Self, that adult, clear conduit to our True Ground that shows us that we are not only able to handle everything, but at the same time we can *experience a growing sense of gratitude, which I believe, when all is said and done, is the greatest practice of all.*

Who is Tony?

Dr. Stultz is an Internationally recognized expert on the practice of Mindfulness. He is founder and Director of the Blue Lotus School of Mindfulness Arts (1999), the Center for Mindful Living (2004), creator of the Four Directions System of Mindfulness (1998) and the Blue Lotus School of Mindful Martial Arts (1999). He is a Fellow of the American Psychotherapy Association, and author of numerous popular and academic works on the practice of Mindful Living, including the award winning book, *Free Your Mind: The Four Directions of an Awakened Life* (2007). In 2017 he released a special version of the book entitled, *Free Your Mind: The Four Directions System of Mindfulness,* for corporate clientele.

He has presented his unique *Four Directions System of Mindfulness*™ at both Harvard and Oxford. His method has helped both individuals and groups in a variety of settings, including hospitals, prisons, universities, non-profits and corporations. His national service includes working the families of victims of the September 2001 Flight 93 tragedy and First Responder victims of Ground Zero. In 2013 he received the World Affairs Council *Torch of Global Enlightenment Award.*

Made in the USA
Middletown, DE
29 November 2022